THE
HOLY
SPIRIT

Philip O. Akinyemi

All Scriptures are from the King James Version of the Bible, unless otherwise stated.® Scripture quotations marked "NKJV" are taken from the New King James Version. Copyright © 1982 by Thomas Nelson, Inc. Used by permission. All rights reserved.

Scripture quotations marked (NIV) are taken from the Holy Bible, New International Version®, NIV®. Copyright © 1973, 1978, 1984 by Biblica, Inc.™ Used by permission of Zondervan. All rights reserved worldwide.

Scripture quotations marked Amplified are taken from the Amplified Bible copyright 1987 by Zondervan Corporation, and the Lockman Foundation.

The excerpt on pages 64-65 was taken from Our Daily Bread®, Copyright 2013 by Our Daily Bread Ministries, Grand Rapids, MI. Used by permission. All rights reserved.

THE HOLY SPIRIT
Copyright © 2016 Philip O. Akinyemi

All rights reserved. No part of this publication may be reproduced, stored in a retrieval system, or transmitted in any form or by any means, electronic, mechanical, photocopying, recording, or otherwise, without the prior written permission of the author.

Author's Contact Email:
feedmypeope365@gmail.com

ISBN: 978-1-7342603-5-9

Visit the author's website at:
www.philipakinyemi.com

Cover design: Jay Cookingham

Printed in the United States of America

Dedication

To the cherished memory of my beloved wife Rachel Omolola Akinyemi, who departed this world on January 18, 2013, to be present before our Lord Jesus Christ. You will always be missed until we meet again.

Acknowledgement

I wish to express my profound gratitude to Dr. Joseph Olarewaju, who read the manuscript, offered suggestions, and wrote the foreword to this book.

My special thanks to my son Joshua, who gave me free accommodation during my writing of this book, which has given me the financial advantage of publishing this book. The blessing of God shall remain with you.

Table of Contents

Foreword 11
Introduction 15
Chapter 1 The Holy Spirit 19
    Who Is the Holy Spirit? 19
    The Holy Spirit as a Person 19
        He Has Knowledge: 19
        He Has Emotions: 20
        He Has Will: 20
    The Actions of the Holy Spirit Fit a Person 21
        The Holy Spirit Leads: 22
        He Intercedes: 25
    Others React to Him as a Person 25
    He Relates as a Person to Others 25
    What Type of Person? 26
    Names (Appellations) 26
    Attributes 27

Chapter 2 The Works (Roles) of the Holy Spirit ... 31
    Creation 31
    Authorship of the Bible 33
    Dealings with People in the Old Testament 34

    Dealings with People in the New Testament 34
        With Unbelievers 35
        With Believers 39

Chapter 3 The Work of the Holy Spirit in the Life of Jesus Christ 45
    Virgin Birth 45
    Jesus Lived a Life Full of the Holy Spirit 46
    Christ's Anointing 46
    Jesus' Temptation (A Proving Ground) 47
    Miracles 54
    His Resurrection 54

Chapter 4 Another Comforter 57
    Advocate 58
    Counselor 59
    Teacher 61
    Comforter 63
    Intercessor 66
    Helper 69

Chapter 5 Baptism with the Holy Spirit 73
    What Is Baptism with the Holy Spirit? 75
    Some Designations Used in the Bible for Baptism with the Holy Spirit 76
    Water Baptism versus Holy Spirit Baptism 76
    The Effect of Baptism on Evangelism 80

You Have to Accept the Promise 81
Receiving Baptism with the Holy Spirit and Holiness
.... 82
Necessity of Baptism with the Holy Spirit 82
Speaking in Tongues: Is It for Today? 84
How to Receive the Baptism of the Holy Spirit.. 85

Chapter 6 The Gifts of the Spirit 87
   The Word of Wisdom 91
   The Word of Knowledge 95
   The Discerning of Spirits 96
   The Gift of Faith 98
   The Working of Miracles 105
   The Gifts of Healing 108
   Prophecy 111
   Divers Kinds of Tongues 112
   Interpretation of Tongues 114

Chapter 7 The Fruit of the Spirit 117
   Love 119
   Joy 122
   Peace 124
   Patience (Longsuffering) 126
   Kindness 129
   Goodness 132
   Faithfulness 134

Gentleness 137
Self-Control.. 139

Foreword

This book is not only timely: it is also highly refreshing. It brings a clear message from the throne for a time like this. The Lord God spoke concerning these days of the latter rain in which we live, saying: *"It shall come to pass afterward, that I will pour out my spirit upon all flesh; and your sons and your daughters shall prophesy, your old men shall dream dreams, your young men shall see visions: And also upon the servants and upon the handmaids in those days will I pour out my spirit"* (Joel 2:28-29). This mighty outpouring that the prophet spoke about, which started on the day of Pentecost and was followed by several showers and seasons of refreshing, is reaching its consummation in these end-times. Our Father God is therefore refreshing us with the fundamentals of the supernatural for our individual lives and for the Body of Christ, the Anointed One.

The book begins by introducing the reader to the Person of the Holy Spirit, the third Person of the triune God. Our brother discusses the ministry of the Holy Spirit in the Old Covenant economy when He came upon prophets, judges, and kings of Israel, contrasting this with His ministry in the New Creation. He introduces readers to the Person of the Holy Spirit through His names, personality, attributes, and character. From the second chapter on, my brother expands on the works of the Holy Spirit in the lives of the unbelievers, and to a greater extent in the lives of the regenerated ones, within whom He resides. He begins with the promise our Master left us as He was finishing His earthly mission and about to ascend on high: *"Nevertheless I tell you the truth; It is expedient for you that I go away: for if I go not away, the **Comforter** will not come unto you; but if I depart, I will send him unto you. . . . Howbeit when he, the Spirit of truth, is come, he will guide you into all truth: for he shall not speak of himself; but whatsoever he shall hear, that shall he speak: and he will shew you things to come"* (John 16:7, 13).

Using these words from the Lord Jesus, and looking a little closer at the meaning of the Greek word *parakletos,* translated to English as "comforter," he step-by-step discusses the ministry of the Holy Spirit in our lives as Advocate, Teacher, Counselor, Intercessor, and Helper. The book gives a clear, comprehensive, and yet concise teaching on manifestations of the Spirit in our lives, covering revelation gifts, power gifts, and utterance gifts in the church of Jesus Christ. He does not leave out the fact that the Holy Spirit helps us pray according to the will of God and bear the fruit of the Spirit, for He is the Vine and we are the branches. Whether you're a new believer still struggling with the baptism of the Holy Spirit, or a believer who's been filled with the Spirit for a while, this book is a must-read. It will enlighten and inspire the new believer and refresh the Holy-Ghost-filled believer.

His core admonition in this book is that we should, like Jesus, depend totally on the Holy Spirit in everything, submit to His rule in our lives, fight with the sword of the Spirit, and pray always in the Holy Ghost. We are to turn to Him, our resident Helper, at all times, whether it be for guidance, for physical or financial needs, to pray correctly, with respect to bearing fruit, or even concerning manifestations of spiritual gifts. We should totally submit to and depend on the Holy Spirit, who is our divine Help from within. He admonishes us to join Paul in praying that God *"would grant* [us], *according to the riches of His glory, to be strengthened with might through* **His Spirit** *in the inner man,"* because our strength to overcome our challenges in this life can only come from the Helper within.

Today, more than ever before, we the church of Jesus Christ are at a crossroads where we need the full manifestation of the Holy Spirit in and through us, both to shine forth the light and character of the Spirit and to demonstrate His spectacular wonders to the world for the glory of God. The branches must bear fruit to the glory of God and for the benefit of this present world. The testimony of Jesus must be declared to this world through the lives and character of the members of His Body. The supernatural and the spectacular operations of the Holy Spirit must be displayed to consummate all things and show to principalities and powers the manifold wisdom of God. The Lord God will use this book to sow the seed to this end in the hearts of all that read it. *The zeal of the Lord of Hosts will perform it.*

Joseph Olarewaju
Dallas, Texas

Introduction

A few months before my wife departed this world to be present with the Lord, I found myself studying more on the Holy Spirit; little did I know that God was preparing me for what was ahead. Before our Lord went to the cross for humanity, He promised His disciples another Comforter: the Holy Spirit, who will abide with us forever and comfort us in all our sorrows. Since my wife's departure on January 18, 2013, the Holy Spirit has been my loving and faithful Comforter.

When it dawned on my spirit to write a book on the Holy Spirit, I debated what I could write that great men of God like Rev. Kenneth E. Hagin, Charles Spurgeon, R. A. Torrey, Howard Carter, and others hadn't written. But I heard in my spirit, "I want to read yours too." As a father, I know, no matter how many children you have, your delight is to hear from each of them, both the great and the small. This has been my inspiration in writing this book.

I have known the Holy Spirit since my late teens, not just by study, but experientially for many years now. I have found over the years that the least understood part of the Godhead is the Holy Spirit, and the reasons are not farfetched: (1) people can easily relate to God the Father because we see fathers around us, and to God the Son because we see sons too; (2) I believe the church is not teaching as much on the Holy Spirit as on God the Father and God the Son.

Since many people are still ignorant of who the Holy Spirit is, when you talk about Him, some simply think of "ghosts" or "spirits" and are scared. They often say, "I don't believe in ghosts or spirits because I have not seen one." A simple question to ask this group of people is "Do you have a brain?" Their response is quick. "Of course I do. If I didn't have a brain, how could I be speaking with you?" But if you go further to ask them if they have ever seen their brain, the answer is an obvious "No!" God is Spirit, and you don't see Him with your physical eyes. *"God is a Spirit: and they that worship him must worship him in spirit and in truth"* (John 4:24).

There are those who say, "I don't want to act funny," because they have seen people run around or even jump on pews in a Holy Ghost meeting. You do not have to run around when the power of the Holy Spirit comes on you. But remember, making fun of people on the reception of the Holy Spirit didn't just start today; it has been so from its inception. On the day of Pentecost, when the first apostles and others gathered together in one place, they were all filled with the Holy Spirit and began to speak in other tongues as the Spirit enabled them. Then some began to mock, saying they were full of new wine. But Peter told them: *"Ye men of Judaea, and all ye that dwell at Jerusalem, be this known unto you, and hearken to my words: For these are not drunken, as ye suppose, seeing it is but the third hour of the day. But this is that which was spoken by the prophet Joel"* (Acts 2:15-16). All you have to do is open your heart and welcome Him in, just as you did when you accepted the Lord Jesus Christ.

Some also think of the Holy Spirit as a bird. I can remember, when I was a boy back in my hometown in Nigeria, in the night we sometimes saw and heard birds with peculiar sounds. This was very scary to children, and we were told that the sound was because witches and wizards were going for a meeting. The birds served as a medium for the evil spirits; they were not birds. However, while we are told in Matthew 3:16 that the Spirit of God descended as a dove upon Jesus after His baptism in the River Jordan, that does not mean the Holy Spirit is a dove. It says "as a dove," not that He is a dove.

There are still those who think of the Holy Spirit as a divine power. This group of people believes that God rewards them with this power for their righteous acts and they can use the power as they will. You often hear them say, "Don't mess with me, or else fire will come down on you," just as Elijah commanded fire to come down on the messengers of the king of Samaria. The power of the Holy Spirit is not a reward. Believing this will lead to pride and self-righteousness. You cannot use the power of the Holy Spirit as you will. The Holy Spirit works in us and through us as He wills. Remember, Simon thought he could purchase the power of the Holy Spirit with money so that whomsoever he laid hands on as he willed would receive the Holy Spirit. Hear what Peter told him: *"Thy money perish with thee, because thou hast thought that the gift of God may be purchased with money. Thou hast neither part nor lot in this matter: for thy heart is not right in the sight of God. Repent therefore of this thy wickedness, and pray God, if perhaps the thought of thine heart may be forgiven thee"* (Acts 8:20-22).

You may wonder why anyone who calls himself a believer would doubt the personality of the Holy Spirit; at the close of most church gatherings, the minister pronounces what is known as "benediction" or "grace," which goes like this: "May the grace of our Lord Jesus Christ, and the love of God, and the sweet fellowship of the Holy Spirit be with you all. Amen." In this statement, there are three Persons mentioned, and that is the Triune God or Godhead. However, after repeating this for many years, most people pay no attention to what they say, hear, or repeat.

The denial of the personality of the Holy Spirit has occurred throughout church history. Even today, the Unitarians and liberals deny His personality and simply consider Him a personification of power. If He is a personification of power, then Satan would be a personification of evil, but even a child knows that Satan exists.

Another source of confusion about the Holy Spirit is the fact that some who are trying to teach or explain His operation or His character do not know Him personally or experientially. Any attempt to explain the Holy Spirit without an understanding of His character and the ways He operates will invariably lead to distortion of that character. How are you going to teach calculus without an understanding of differentiation and integration? No wonder some people are uncomfortable when you talk about the Holy Spirit.

Keeping people ignorant of the Holy Spirit has always been the goal of Satan. This ignorance robs Christians of their potential to carry out great exploits for God (Daniel 11:32). It also robs the Holy Spirit of the adoration, worship, and love due Him because we do not recognize Him as a real Person who is infinitely wise, and not just a power that we can use as we desire. Jesus told His disciples to tarry in Jerusalem until they were endued with power. *"But ye shall receive power, after that the Holy Ghost is come upon you: and ye shall be witnesses unto me both in Jerusalem, and in all Judaea, and in Samaria, and unto the uttermost part of the earth"* (Acts 1:8). To effectively carry out our assignment for God in this life, we must totally depend on the Holy Spirit.

We shall study who the Holy Spirit is, His roles, His baptism, and the gifts and the fruit of the Spirit. My prayer is that the Lord will, through the Holy Spirit, use this book to bring the true knowledge of Him to you.

Chapter 1

The Holy Spirit

Who Is the Holy Spirit?

The Holy Spirit is the Third Person of the triune God. He is a divine Person, so you do not refer to Him as "it." The Holy Spirit is also referred to as the Holy Ghost. When we say the Holy Spirit is a Person, we are not saying that He has hands, legs, eyes, or other human bodily parts; these do not describe the attributes of a person, but corporeity. A human being lacking hands or feet does not make him less than a person. A person, whether young or old, tall or short, rich or poor, male or female, must exhibit these attributes: (1) intelligence or knowledge, (2) emotion or feeling, and (3) will. A day-old child has intelligence, emotion, and will. If the mother puts her breast in his mouth, he draws it with no instruction. If the surroundings are too hot or cold, he shows his feelings. When he is hungry, he shows his emotion by crying. If a child doesn't want to sleep, you may force him to close his eyes, but that does not mean he is sleeping, because he has a will. The Holy Spirit is intelligent. He is not a force that is available for you to use as you want.

The Holy Spirit as a Person

He Has Knowledge:

In 1 Corinthians 2:10-11, we read, *"But God hath revealed them unto us by his Spirit: for the Spirit searcheth all things, yea, the deep things of God. For what man knoweth the things of a man, save the spirit of man which is in him? even so the things of God knoweth no man, but the Spirit of God."*

In this passage we are told that the Spirit searches the deep things of God and He knows the things of God. Right away, you cannot say the Holy Spirit is an influence or a force or even a personification of power. A force cannot search or know things.

Again, let us look at Romans 8:27, *"And he that searcheth the hearts knoweth what is the mind of the Spirit, because he maketh intercession for the saints according to the will of God."* Here we see that the Holy Spirit has a mind. And the Greek word used here is the same as in Romans 8:7, which carries an idea or thought. It should gladden the believer's heart that the Holy Spirit, who knows the thoughts of the Father, makes intercession for us according to the will of God. He modifies our prayers and lines them up with the will of the Father. Praise God! No wonder Paul said, *"We do not know what we should pray for as we ought: but the Spirit Himself makes intercession for us with groanings which cannot be uttered"* (Romans 8:26).

He Has Emotions:

Paul tells us not to grieve the Holy Spirit. Remember, he was writing to believers in Ephesus at that time. *"And do not grieve the Holy Spirit of God, by whom you were sealed for the day of redemption"* (Ephesians 4:30). We all know that an influence cannot grieve, but the Holy Spirit grieves when we as believers continue in sin. Therefore, we must run away from any appearance of evil so as not to offend Him.

He Has Will:

We are told that the Holy Spirit distributes gifts to each one individually as He wills (1 Corinthians 12:11). In Acts 16:6-7 we read, *"Now when they had gone throughout Phrygia and the region of Galatia, and were forbidden of the Holy Ghost to preach the word in Asia, After they were come to Mysia, they assayed to go into Bithynia: but the Spirit suffered them not."* Here we see the Holy Spirit forbidding Paul and his team from going to Asia to preach, though it was for a noble cause. The all-knowing Holy Spirit has a plan. His will must be obeyed if we want to be successful.

From the foregoing, the Holy Spirit possesses intelligence, emotion, and will; therefore, He must be a Person.

The Actions of the Holy Spirit Fit a Person

The Holy Spirit's actions also show that He is a Person: He (1) speaks, (2) guides, (3) intercedes, (4) convicts, and (5) performs miracles. These actions cannot be done by a force or influence, but are done by a Person.

In Revelation 2:7 we read, *"He that hath an ear, let him hear what the Spirit saith unto the churches; To him that overcometh will I give to eat of the tree of life, which is in the midst of the paradise of God."* The Holy Spirit is here speaking to the seven churches in Asia, but it is relevant to the Body of Christ today. These sayings are not an impersonal enlightenment that comes to our minds, but the words of a Person with knowledge of what happened and what lies ahead. An influence can't do that.

These verses of Scripture also attest to the personhood of the Holy Spirit: *"The Spirit of the LORD spake by me, and his word was in my tongue"* (2 Samuel 23:2). *"And the Spirit of the LORD fell upon me, and said unto me, Speak; Thus saith the LORD; Thus have ye said, O house of Israel: for I know the things that come into your mind, every one of them"* (Ezekiel 11:5). *"For it is not ye that speak, but the Spirit of your Father which speaketh in you"* (Matthew 10:20). *"Then the Spirit said unto Philip, Go near, and join thyself to this chariot"* (Acts 8:29). *"While Peter thought on the vision, the Spirit said unto him, Behold, three men seek thee"* (Acts 10:19).

The Holy Spirit Leads:

The Psalmist says of God, *"Your Spirit is good; lead me"* (Psalm 143:10, NKJV). As a young man, I was led by the Holy Spirit to Jos, a city in northern Nigeria, for a job opportunity. Before graduating from a technical school, I had been admitted to United Missionary Theological College, Ilorin (Nigeria), along with a dear friend, McDonald Kure, to start the bachelor's degree program in theology in 1970. Close to the date of resumption, I still could not get financial support, and I knew it was not going to be possible for me to join the program. I was sad and disappointed, but made a simple prayer unto God and asked, "What do I do next?" Just as I finished praying, I heard in my spirit, "Go to Jos." Jos was then the capital city of Benue-Plateau state in northern Nigeria—a beautiful city with good weather year-round.

In January 1970, I headed to Jos, not knowing where I would stay. I remembered a dear brother in Christ by the name of Christopher Aiyeru, who was a year ahead of me in technical school, and was working in Jos. He had sent some amount to the Fellowship of Christian Students (FCS), of which I was part of the leadership. So I decided I would look for him and see if he would be kind enough to let me stay with him. At this time the main means of communication was writing letters, and they were sometimes never received (it was not the era of emails or cell phones, and even then a LAN phone line was as rare as gold). Without prior notice, I said to myself I could lodge with him. I had no idea how much staying in a hotel or motel would cost. It was not even a consideration; that was how naïve I was. When I left my hometown, Iyah-Gbedde, all I had was seven British pounds that my father gave me.

The cheapest means of traveling then was by train, so I took the train from Ilorin to Kaduna, because there was no direct train to Jos. Everyone had to stop at Kaduna Junction.

Kaduna was a large city and was for a time the capital city of the then Northern Region. At Kaduna, I had to stay the night with my nephew, Kayode Abodunde, a soldier. He encouraged me to stay with him in Kaduna and look for a job, since there was no relative living in Jos, but I said my heart was in Jos.

The following day I left for Jos by bus, which was about a four-hour drive. From the bus station, I went directly to look for Christopher, who was working at Niger Motors, a subsidiary of United African Corporation. When I got there, I was told he had traveled out of town. But the Holy Spirit who directed me to Jos had a way out: another fine brother in the Lord called Sam said, "Why don't you come and stay with me overnight?" I was glad and blessed the Lord for the favor.

The following morning, as Sam was ready to go to work, I prepared and went with him. Jos is on a plateau and generally cold for an average Nigerian; it was too chilly for me as I took my shower in the morning. While at Niger Motors, I learned that a vice president from Lagos was visiting the branch. I asked the service manager to let me talk with the visiting vice president. He reluctantly allowed me. So, as he was walking through the vehicle section, I approached him, introduced myself, and asked for a job. He then turned to the service manager, a Ghanaian, and asked if he could offer me a position. He said they had just taken two students from a nearby technical school, and there was no opening for me in Jos. The vice president told him to write a note for me to take to the Kaduna branch in case they had an opening there. I got the note and traveled back to Kaduna the same day.

This was wonderful to me, because there was a branch in Kano, another large city in northern Nigeria, and he could have given me a note to go to Kano, but I had no relative there that I could stay with. At that time I probably had less than five pounds on me, so going back to Kaduna, where I had a relative, was a great blessing from God.

The following day, I went to the Kaduna branch of Niger Motors and took the note to the service manager, a Briton. On reading the note, he said, "I will give you a test." The test was on math and auto technology. Being fresh from school, I got every question on the test right. He was surprised and took my paper to the branch manager, another Briton. That same day, he laid off two temporary workers and asked me to start work the following day. Two students had been hired as trainees and given scholarships for further education at Kaduna Polytechnic, but were required to do a medical test. Unfortunately for one of them, his test reported that he had gonorrhea, so the service manager fired him immediately, and gave me his position as trainee with his scholarship in the same week.

I told this story to show you that the Holy Spirit leads and guides His own people through our human spirit. The Bible says, *"The spirit of man is the candle of the LORD, searching all the inward parts of the belly"* (Proverbs 20:27). The Holy Spirit told my spirit to go to Jos. If I had stopped at Kaduna, where I had relatives, I would have missed this lifetime opportunity. Staying at Kaduna made more sense to the human mind, but with God, you don't lean on your own reasoning or intellect. God is Spirit, and He deals with us in our spirits. God has promised in His Word, *"I will instruct you and teach you in the way you should go; I will guide you with My eye"* (Psalm 32:8, NKJV).

My friend, you need the Holy Spirit to guide you through this life's journey. When it looks dark, He is there to lead you. He knows the way through the wilderness. He led Israel by the right way that they might go to a city of habitation (Psalm 107:7).

He Intercedes:

The Holy Spirit intercedes for the believer. This can be seen in Romans 8:26: *"The Spirit Himself makes intercession for us with groanings which cannot be uttered."* Jesus also talks about the Holy Spirit guiding us into all truth (John 16:13). He convicts the world of sin and of righteousness, and of judgment (John 16:8). He spoke to Peter and delegated him to the house of Cornelius (Acts 10:19-21). While the disciples ministered unto the Lord, we are told the Holy Spirit spoke and said, *"Separate me Barnabas and Saul for the work whereunto I have called them"* (Acts 13:2). And in the case of Philip, the Holy Spirit performed a miracle by taking him away from the Ethiopian eunuch (Acts 8:39).

These activities obviously cannot be done by a force or influence; we see again through His activities that the Holy Spirit is a Person.

Others React to Him as a Person

The Holy Spirit can be blasphemed against (Matthew 12:31). People can also lie to the Holy Spirit. An example is the story of Ananias and his wife (Acts 5:3). We are told in Ephesians 4:30 not to grieve the Holy Spirit. He can also be resisted, as we see in Acts 7:51: *"You always resist the Holy Spirit; as your fathers did, so do you."* To think of acting and reacting to an influence or force in these ways is absurd; you can only do these things to a person.

He Relates as a Person to Others

The Holy Spirit related to the apostles in a manner that shows His own distinct personality. In

Acts 15:28 we read, *"For it seemed good to the Holy Ghost, and to us, to lay upon you no greater burden than these necessary things."* He also relates to the Lord Jesus in such a way that if the Lord is a Person, one must conclude that the Holy Spirit is also. In John 16:14, Jesus said, *"He will glorify Me, for He will take of what is Mine and declare it to you."*

To other Trinity Members, He relates as an equal Person. *"Go therefore and make disciples of all the nations, baptizing them in the name of the Father and of the Son and of the Holy Spirit"* (Matthew 28:19). Also in 2 Corinthians 13:14, *"The grace of the Lord Jesus Christ, and the love of God, and the communion of the Holy Spirit be with you all. Amen."* And in 1 John 5:7, *"For there are three that bear record in heaven, the Father, the Word, and the Holy Spirit: and these three are one."*

What Type of Person?

As shown earlier in our study, the Holy Spirit is a Person distinct from God the Father and God the Son. Now, what kind of Person is He? That will be our consideration here. In Scripture, His appellations or names, His actions, and His associations with the Father and Jesus Christ show us that He is divine. The proof of His divinity will also confirm His personality, because if the Holy Spirit is equally God, then the Holy Spirit is also a Person.

Names (Appellations)

From the Old Testament to the New Testament, the Holy Spirit is related by name to the other two Persons of the Trinity.

The Old Testament:

1. "The Spirit of God" (Genesis 1:2),
2. "My spirit" (Genesis 6:3),
3. "The Spirit of the Lord" (Judges 6:34; 2 Samuel 23:2),
4. "The good spirit" (Nehemiah 9:20),
5. "Thy holy spirit" (Psalm 51:11),
6. "The Spirit of the Lord God" (Isaiah 61:1),
7. "The spirit" (Ezekiel 2:2).

The New Testament:

1. "Spirit of God" (Matthew 3:16),
2. "The Spirit" (Matthew 4:1),
3. "The Spirit of your Father" (Matthew 10:20),
4. "My spirit" (Matthew 12:18),
5. "The Spirit of the Lord" (Luke 4:18),
6. "The Holy Spirit" (Luke 11:13),
7. "Comforter" (John 14:16),
8. "The Spirit of truth" (John 14:17),
9. "Spirit of holiness" (Romans 1:4),
10. "Spirit of Christ" (Romans 8:9),
11. "Spirit of his Son" (Galatians 4:6),
12. "The holy Spirit of promise" (Ephesians 1:13),
13. "The holy Spirit of God" (Ephesians 4:30),
14. "The eternal Spirit" (Hebrews 9:14),
15. "The seven Spirits of God" (Revelation 3:1).

Attributes

Almost anyone who believes in God will confidently tell you that God is all-knowing, He is powerful, He is everywhere, and He is eternal. That is to say, He is omniscient, omnipresent, and omnipotent, and He is eternal. All these attributes are ascribed to the Holy Spirit.

Omnipresence:

Psalm 139:7-12: *"Whither shall I go from thy spirit? Or whither shall I flee from thy presence? If I ascend up into heaven, thou art there: if I make my bed in hell, behold, thou art there. If I take the wings of the morning, and dwell in the uttermost parts of the sea; even there shall thy hand lead me, and thy right hand shall hold me. If I say, surely the darkness shall cover me; even the night shall be light about me. Yea, the darkness hideth not from thee; but the night shineth as the day: the darkness and the light are both alike to thee."*

Omniscience:

The Holy Spirit is all-knowing and no one teaches Him, as seen in Isaiah 40:13-14, *"Who hath directed the Spirit of the LORD, or being his counselor hath taught him? With whom took he counsel, and who instructed him, and taught him in the path of judgment, and taught him knowledge, and shewed to him the way of understanding?"* Because He knows all things, He will also teach us all things, as seen in John 14:26: *"But the Comforter, which is the Holy Ghost, whom the Father will send in my name, he shall teach you all things, and bring all things to your remembrance, whatsoever I have said unto you."*

Omnipotence:

By virtue of His work in creation, He is all-powerful. Psalm 104:30: *"Thou sendest forth thy spirit, they are created: and thou renewest the face of the earth."* Also, the formation of our Lord's body in a virgin's womb was by the power of the Holy Spirit. Luke 1:35: *"And the angel answered and said unto her, The Holy Ghost shall come upon thee, and the power of the Highest shall overshadow thee: therefore also that holy thing which shall be born of thee shall be called the Son of God."* Paul tells us that mighty signs and wonders happened because of the power of the Holy Spirit. Romans 15:19: *"Through mighty signs and wonders, by the power of the Spirit of God; so that from Jerusalem, and round about unto Illyricum, I have fully preached the gospel of Christ."*

Eternity:

The Holy Spirit is eternal, as seen in Hebrews 9:14: *"How much more shall the blood of Christ, who through the eternal Spirit offered himself without spot to God, purge your conscience from dead works to serve the living God?"*

Truth:

He is also ascribed the attribute of truth, as seen in John 15:26: *"But when the Comforter is come, whom I will send unto you from the Father, even the Spirit of truth, which proceedeth from the Father, he shall testify of me."*

Since all these divine attributes are ascribed to the Holy Spirit, He must be divine.

Chapter 2

The Works (Roles) of the Holy Spirit

Creation

Over the centuries, philosophers and theologians alike have used the cosmological argument for the existence of a First Cause or an Uncaused Cause who created the universe. Ancient Greeks like Plato and Aristotle argued that the universe was brought into existence by God. The evolutionists in their confusion theorized that "The Big Bang" was responsible for physical matter in the universe, and the atheists in their foolishness said there was no God. No wonder the Psalmist said, *"The fool hath said in his heart, there is no God"* (Psalm 14:1).

The account of creation is right before our eyes. The book of Genesis gives the account of creation. Genesis 1:1 tells us, *"In the beginning God created the heaven and the earth."* As we go further in the chapter, God said, *"Let us make man in our image, after our likeness"* (v. 26). The Hebrew *Elohiym* (God) used here is in the plural form, thereby introducing to us God the Father, God the Son, and God the Holy Spirit; all were present at creation. One of the verses in the New Testament that makes the Triune God very clear to us is John 14:26, where Jesus said, *"But the Comforter, which is the Holy Spirit, whom the Father will send in my name, he shall teach you all things, and bring all things to your remembrance, whatsoever I have said unto you."*

God the Father, God the Son, and God the Holy Spirit have one purpose, but play unique roles. As another example of this, take Ford Motor Company, which has many departments, such as design, manufacturing, assembly, finance, and others. The company has a main goal, and that is to make good and reliable vehicles that will please the customers, but each department has different roles, and they may overlap in achieving the goal. The triune God has one purpose, but they play different roles in achieving that goal, and sometimes the roles of the Three might overlap.

The works of creation is usually ascribed to the Deity (God the Father, God the Son, and God the Holy Spirit). However, the Scriptures specifically ascribe some things to individuals. Someone has compared the role of the Father in creation to that of an architect who comes up with the blueprints, while the Son is like a foreman who directs what needs to be done, and the Holy Spirit is the craftsman who takes the materials in hand and shapes them to the proper form. Job tells us, *"By his Spirit he hath garnished the heavens; his hand hath formed the crooked serpent"* (Job 26:13). In Genesis we are also told that the earth was without form, and void; and darkness was upon the face of the deep; and the Spirit of God moved upon the face of the waters (Genesis 1:2).

Astronomers estimate that there are 200 billion to 400 billion stars within the Milky Way—all garnished and put in their rightful positions by the Holy Spirit. Imagine if the sun, which is about 93 million miles (150 million kilometers) from our planet, was put much closer; it would have destroyed all living things with its energy. But the omniscient Holy Spirit positioned it in its rightful location so that it does not hurt us.

Job describes the wisdom and strength of the Holy Spirit in chapter 9:4-9 (NIV): *"His wisdom is profound, his power is vast. Who has resisted him and come out unscathed? He moves mountains without their knowing it and overturns them in his anger. He shakes the earth from its place and makes its pillars tremble. He speaks to the sun and it does not shine; he seals off the light of the stars. He alone stretches out the heavens and treads on the waves of the sea. He is the Maker of the Bear and Orion, the Pleiades and the constellations of the south. He performs wonders that cannot be fathomed, miracles that cannot be counted."*

Another realm of creation that is the work of the Holy Spirit is the creation of man and animals with their births and generations. In Psalm 104:29-30 we read, *"Thou hidest thy face, they are troubled: thou takest away their breath, they die, and return to their dust. Thou sendest forth thy spirit, they are created: and thou renewest the face of the earth."* As far as we have come in science today with in vitro fertilization, without the Spirit of God all would avail to nothing, because the creation of all life and flesh is His handiwork.

Authorship of the Bible

The Holy Spirit was the Agent for the authorship of the Bible. Peter stated that the prophecy never came by the will of man, but holy men of God spoke as they were moved by the Holy Spirit (2 Peter 1:21). The New International Version rendering is that the writers were carried along by the Holy Spirit, while 2 Samuel 23:2 and Micah 3:8 indicate that the prophets spoke by means of the Holy Spirit.

In speaking with the Pharisees, Jesus quoted from Psalm 110, which He acknowledged was written by David through the Spirit (Matthew 22:43). Peter quoted from Psalm 41 with regard to the replacement of Judas, *"Men and brethren, this Scripture had to be fulfilled, which the Holy Spirit spoke before by the mouth of David concerning Judas, who became a guide to those who arrested Jesus"* (Acts 1:16). Paul also quoted from Isaiah 6:9 when he expounded and testified about the kingdom of God to the Jews in Rome (Acts 28:26-28).

Dealings with People in the Old Testament

The ministry of the Holy Spirit to people in the Old Testament is quite sparse compared to His dealings with people in the New Testament. This is due to the fact that the Holy Spirit lives within believers under the New Covenant.

In the Old Testament, the Holy Spirit came upon specific people like prophets, kings, or judges. But from the day of Pentecost onwards, the Holy Spirit has been poured on believers. Joel 2:29 says, *"And also on My menservants and on My maidservants I will pour out My Spirit in those days."*

Moses was a man of God who had the Spirit of God upon him. When Moses needed help with the children of Israel he was leading to the land of promise, God took the Spirit that was upon him and placed it upon the seventy elders; and when the Spirit rested upon them, they prophesied (Numbers 11:25). Joseph had the Spirit of God upon him (Genesis 41:38). Joshua the son of Nun, who took over the leadership after Moses' death, had the Spirit upon him (Numbers 27:18). Bezalel was filled with the spirit of God for the wisdom, understanding, and knowledge he needed in building the Ark of God (Exodus 31:3). Samson, who was one of the judges (leaders) of Israel before they started having kings, had the Spirit of God upon him (Judges 13:25). The Spirit of God came upon the prophets and King Saul and David (1 Samuel 10:10; 16:13). This illustrates the need for the Holy Spirit to successfully carry out any endeavor that God has for us.

Dealings with People in the New Testament

"Nevertheless I tell you the truth; It is expedient for you that I go away: for if I go not away, the Comforter will not come unto you; but if I depart, I will send him unto you. And when he is come, he will reprove the world of sin, and of righteousness, and of judgment: Of sin, because they

believe not on me; Of righteousness, because I go to my Father, and ye see me no more; Of judgment, because the prince of this world is judged" (John 16:7-11).

The Lord said this when the time drew nearer for Him to go to the cross for humanity. He told His disciples three important things that the Holy Spirit would do when He comes: (1) convict the world of sin for not believing in Him, (2) convict the world of righteousness because Christ went to His Father in heaven, and (3) convict the world of judgment because the ruler of this world (Satan) would be judged.

With Unbelievers

Conviction of Sin:

It is the work of the Holy Spirit to convict the world of sin. Note Jesus did not say sins, but sin: it is the sin of unbelief. Some people trust in their good works to get to heaven, and no matter what you say to them, they think they are good. They consider themselves better than others because they do not commit adultery, fornicate, smoke, or steal. They do not know that all our righteousness is as filthy rags (Isaiah 64:6). Our good works cannot save us. It's God's work in sending His only begotten Son that saves us when we believe in Him. And until the Holy Spirit convinces such people through the instrumentation of the Word of God that all have sinned and come short of the glory of God, they do not see the need to turn to Jesus. It is like a swimmer who thinks he can swim across Lake Michigan, but when he gets halfway, finds he has no more strength to swim. He comes to his wits' end. He becomes aware that if he does not get help, he might drown and die; then he calls for help.

Have you witnessed to someone who seems to have good head knowledge of the Bible and thus argues and counters whatever you tell him from the Word of God? Don't be discouraged or feel bad. Remember, as brilliant and eloquent as Paul was, he could not convict King Agrippa. He said to Paul, *"You almost persuade me to become a Christian"* (Acts 26:28). Our assignment is to sow the seed—the Word of God—but the Holy Spirit is the one that brings conviction. He will convict the world of sin.

After the day of Pentecost, when the disciples received the promise of the Father, the Holy Ghost, Peter stood to tell those people who claimed to be righteous, who saw themselves as the seed of Abraham and felt they were in good standing with God even though it was an automatic inheritance, that salvation is not inherited. You have to come before God as individuals. The fact that your parents are saved and are Christians does not mean you are. You may have early exposure to being a Christian, but you are not one until you accept Christ into your heart as your Lord and Savior.

When Peter preached to these people, the Bible tells us that they were pricked in their hearts. Who did the pricking? It was the Holy Spirit! When the Holy Spirit pricked their hearts, they asked Peter, *"What shall we do?"* (Acts 2:37). Then Peter said unto them, *"Repent, and be baptized every one of you in the name of Jesus Christ for the remission of sins, and ye shall receive the gift of the Holy Spirit. Then they that gladly received his word were baptized: and the same day there were added unto them about three thousand souls"* (Acts 2:38-41). Just in one day, three thousand souls were saved. Hallelujah! This is the work of the Holy Spirit.

I remember many years back in Kaduna, Nigeria. A group of us from the Apostolic Church known as the Evangelical Party went to preach to the local people, called the Gwaris. We spoke in English, and we had an interpreter, Pastor Shehu

Waziri. We preached in turns, and as we were preaching, a man became infuriated with us and went back to his house to get deadly arrows that it was said must not touch human blood. He came back, maybe to aim at those of us he planned to shoot at, but as he stood planning, the Holy Spirit touched his heart. At the end of the preaching that day, he pulled Pastor Waziri aside and confessed what he had intended to do. "Something spoke to me that I must not do it," he said. He then asked for prayer to be saved.

On that day, first, God protected us according to His Word, and second, salvation came to this fellow who had determined to injure or kill us. We must rely on the Holy Spirit to do His work to convince the people we reach out to. No matter how stubborn people's hearts are, the Holy Spirit is able to convince them and open their inner eyes so they see their wretchedness and turn to Christ for salvation.

Conviction of Righteousness:

The Holy Spirit will not only convict the world of sin, but of righteousness, because Jesus was going to His Father. Jesus would soon physically leave the earth, and the Holy Spirit, who replaced Him, would reveal Christ's righteousness in the hearts of the unsaved. Jesus said in John 15:26, *"But when the Comforter is come, whom I will send unto you from the Father, even the Spirit of truth, which proceedeth from the Father, he shall testify of me."* The Holy Spirit, who is the Spirit of Truth, will testify about Jesus and convict man that Christ is the righteous One who was condemned and killed, was raised from the dead, and now sits at the Father's right hand in heaven (Ephesians 1:20). The Holy Spirit will convict unbelievers of the need to take on the righteousness of Christ, for without it you cannot see the glory of God (Romans 3:23).

Conviction of Judgment:

The Holy Spirit will also convict unbelievers of judgment because the prince of this world is judged. The prince of this world is Satan (John 12:31, 14:30, 16:11; Ephesians 2:2). When Jesus went to the cross, it appeared that he was judged and condemned, but it was to put Satan to shame, because Christ defeated him by going to the cross. Sin no longer has dominion over us. In 1 Corinthians 15:55-57, we read: *"O death, where is thy sting? O grave, where is thy victory? The sting of death is sin; and the strength of sin is the law. But thanks are to God, which gives us the victory through our Lord Jesus Christ."*

Those who follow Christ will not share in the eternal damnation that awaits Satan and his angels. Therefore, the Holy Spirit will convict unbelievers of this truth so that they can turn to Christ and be saved and freed from the judgment to come.

The Apostolic Church's second tenet reads: *"The utter depravity of human nature, the necessity for Repentance and Regeneration and the Eternal doom of the finally impenitent."*

The eternal doom is only intended for Satan and his angels, but the unbelieving will share in it. Repentance and regeneration are necessary so that you can reign with Christ forever in His kingdom. The writer of Hebrews reminds us, *"It is appointed unto men once to die, but after this the judgment"* (Hebrews 9:27).

Those who come to Christ and take Him as their Lord and Savior will not be condemned. The Lord makes it plain in John 3:17-18: *"For God sent not his Son into the world to condemn the world; but that the world through him might be saved. He that believeth on him is not condemned: but he that believes not is condemned already, because he has not believed in the name of the only begotten Son of God."*

With Believers

Regeneration:

The regeneration of believers is the work of the Holy Spirit. The word "regeneration" means "new birth, renewal, or recreation." It occurs only twice in the King James Version: first used by our Lord Jesus in Matthew 19:28 and second by Paul in Titus 3:5.

Matthew 19:28 reads, *"And Jesus said unto them, Verily I say unto you, That ye which have followed me, in the regeneration when the Son of man shall sit in the throne of his glory, ye also shall sit upon twelve thrones, judging the twelve tribes of Israel."*

Titus 3:5 reads, *"Not by works of righteousness which we have done, but according to his mercy he saved us, by the washing of regeneration, and renewing of the Holy Ghost."*

The usage of "regeneration" by our Lord Jesus in the above passage takes a broader perspective, describing the rebirth of the new earth, but Paul talks about regeneration of individuals. Jesus talks about the future regeneration when He will set up His kingdom on earth in the coming millennium. The prophets tell us what will happen during this glorious time (Isaiah 2:4, 11; Micah 4:3). Peter calls it the time of *"restitution of all things"* (Acts 3:21). This is the restoration of the original and perfect condition of things that existed before the fall of our first parents, which the Jews looked for in connection with the advent of the Messiah, and which we Christians expect in connection with the visible return of Jesus from heaven.

"Regeneration" in Titus 3:5 refers to the rebirth of believers through the agency of the Holy Spirit. It is not because of our works of righteousness, but by the mercy of God that we receive the regeneration of the Holy Spirit. It is the impartation of God's life or nature to believers. God bestows His own nature upon us and we partake in it (2 Peter 1:4). Jesus calls it being *"born again"* (John 3:3, 7), *"born of God"* (John 1:13). *"Therefore if any man be in Christ, he is a new creature: old things are passed away; behold all things are become new"* (2 Corinthians 5:17). All this is done by the mercy and grace of God. In Ephesians 2:10, we read, *"For we are His workmanship, created in Christ Jesus for good works, which God prepared beforehand that we should walk in them."*

Why the need for regeneration? The Bible teaches us that flesh and blood cannot inherit the kingdom of God (1 Corinthians 15:50). The human race is depraved, wicked, and corrupt. Corruption cannot inherit incorruption, says the Word of God. Sin alienated man from God and His kind of life (Ephesians 2:1, 4:18; Isaiah 59:2). The Bible further tells us that all have sinned and come short of the glory of God (Romans 3:23). And there is none righteous, no, not one (Romans 3:10). The heart of man is equally deceitful above all things, and desperately wicked to the extent that the Bible says, *"Who can know it?"* (Jeremiah 17:9). Hence, we see that we must have a new nature suitable for the kingdom of God. Through the grace of God, by the agency of the Holy Spirit, believers are regenerated.

How does the Holy Spirit do it? Our Lord taught on the subject of being born again in John 3, when a ruler and scholarly Pharisee named Nicodemus came to Him by night. In their discussion, Jesus said unto him, *"Verily, verily, I say unto thee, except a man is born again, he cannot see the kingdom of God. And Nicodemus asked, How can a man be born when he is old? Can he enter the second time into his mother's womb, and be born? Jesus answered, Verily, verily, I say unto thee, except a man be born of water and of the Spirit, he cannot enter into the kingdom of God"* (John 3:3-5).

It was shocking to Nicodemus that Jesus said one had to be born again, and he asked how this could happen. Jesus, the wise teacher, said calmly, "A man has to be born of water and of the Spirit to qualify for the kingdom of God."

Let us examine what the water means. Water in Scripture is sometimes used as a symbol: for example, in John 7:37-39, Jesus spoke of the living water, which he interpreted to be the Holy Spirit. Some have taken the water in the Lord's discussion with Nicodemus to mean water baptism, but this is not true. Being immersed in water does not give you the new birth or God's nature. It does not qualify you for the kingdom of God. Some churches even baptize little children who have not even come to the realization of their sinful nature. Remember, the thief on the cross never had a chance to be water baptized, but when he believed and confessed Jesus Christ, salvation came to him.

The water Jesus was referring to is the Word of God. John 15:3 says, *"You are clean through the word which I have spoken unto you."* The Apostle Peter wrote, *"Having been born again, not of corruptible seed but incorruptible, through the word of God which lives and abides forever"* (1 Peter 1:23). Peter is speaking of the Word of God that has been used in regeneration. The Word of God is the means by which the Holy Spirit accomplishes the new birth. Here, Peter is saying the same thing Jesus said in John 3:5.

Apostle James attributes the sovereign work of God in regeneration to the living Word of God. He writes, *"Of His own will begat He us with the Word of truth"* (James 1:18). Our Lord said, *"The words that I speak unto you, they are spirit, and they are life"* (John 6:63). And, as we have already seen, we are cleaned through the word of Christ. He prayed to the Father, *"Sanctify them through Thy truth; Thy word is truth"* (John 17:17). The Psalmist wrote, *"Wherewithal shall a young man cleanse his way? By taking heed thereto according the Thy Word"* (Psalm 119:9). These passages of Scripture all support the fact that God's Word is the divine means for the regeneration of sinners, and that the "water" in John 3:5 symbolizes the Word of God. In further support of the water and word interpretation of John 3:5, the Apostle Paul described how Christ sanctifies and cleanses His church *"with the washing of water by the word"* (Ephesians 5:26).

To be "born of water and of the Spirit" is to be regenerated by means of the Word of God and by the active agency of the Spirit of God. It is not by the Word of God alone that a man is regenerated, but by the Word and the Holy Spirit: *"by the washing of regeneration, and renewing of the Holy Ghost"* (Titus 3:5).

Indwelling:

Indwelling occurs subsequent to salvation or regeneration, and it is a gift from God to all who are born again (Acts 11:16-17; Romans 5:5; 2 Corinthians 5:5). The indwelling of the Holy Spirit in a believer is foundational to all His ministries. The night before His crucifixion, Jesus made it known to His disciples that He would pray to the Father and send them another Comforter (the Holy Spirit) that would abide in them forever. The Spirit would literally live in them or dwell in them.

The Apostle Paul clearly says that if anyone does not have the Spirit of Christ, the Holy Spirit, he is none of His. *"But you are not in the flesh but in the Spirit, if indeed the Spirit of God dwells in you. Now if anyone does not have the Spirit of Christ, he is not His"* (Romans 8:9). If the Holy Spirit does not have an abode in you, you are definitely not regenerated, and you do not belong to Christ.

Does the Holy Spirit dwell in sinning believers? The answer is a definite yes! Paul, writing to the believers in Corinth, reminded them that they were the temple of God, and that the Holy Spirit dwelt in them (1 Corinthians 3:16). Some Corinthian believers were found living in sin. There was envy, strife, and division within the Christian people (1 Corinthians 3:3), and some among them went to law before the unjust, and not before the saints (1 Corinthians 6). Paul therefore rebuked them, reminding them of the One who dwelt in them—the Holy Spirit. Do we not see the same thing in our churches today? The answer is not farfetched.

Author R. A. Torrey puts it this way, *"The Holy Spirit dwells in every child of God. In some, however, He dwells way back, behind consciousness, in the hidden sanctuary of their spirits, He is not allowed to take possession as He desires of the whole man—spirit, soul and body."* It is time to recognize that the Holy Spirit is in you, as a child of God. You are His temple and you are not your own.

First Corinthians 6:19 says, *"What? Know ye not that your body is the temple of the Holy Spirit which is in you, which ye have of God, and ye are not your own?"* Hear also what God said, *"And what agreement hath the temple of God with idols? for ye are the temple of the living God; as God hath said, I will dwell in them, and walk in them; and I will be their God, and they shall be my people"* (2 Corinthians 6:16).

Benefits of the Indwelling

1. ***Believers are set free from the power of sin.*** In Romans 8:2, we read, *"For the law of the Spirit of life in Christ Jesus hath made me free from the law of sin and death."* Since we have been set free from the power of sin we now can submit to God's law and we are pleasing to God (Romans 8:7-8).

2. ***We have the Living Water that satisfies within us.*** In John 4:14, Jesus told the Samaritan woman by the well, *"But whosoever drinketh of the water that I shall give him shall never*

thirst; but the water that I shall give him shall be in him a well of water springing up into everlasting life." In John 7:37-39, Jesus explained this Living Water to us: *"On the last day, that great day of the feast, Jesus stood and cried out, saying, If anyone thirsts, let him come to Me and drink. He who believes in Me, as the Scripture has said, out of his heart will flow rivers of living water. But this He spoke concerning the Spirit, whom those believing in Him would receive; for the Holy Spirit was not yet given, because Jesus was not yet glorified."*

3. ***It gives us hope for the resurrection of our mortal bodies when Jesus returns.*** Romans 8:11: *"And if the Spirit of him who raised Jesus from the dead is living in you, he who raised Christ from the dead will also give life to your mortal bodies through his Spirit, who lives in you."*

4. ***We are led in the path of God.*** *"For as many as are led by the Spirit of God, they are the sons of God"* (Romans 8:14).

5. ***We become intimate with God.*** We call Him "Abba, Father," that is, "Father, Father" (Romans 8:15). We can come confidently before Him. We realize that we are His children and joint heirs with Jesus Christ, His only begotten Son. Now, hear what the Apostle Paul says in verses 16-17: *"The Spirit himself testifies with our spirit that we are God's children. Now if we are children, then we are heirs—heirs of God and co-heirs with Christ, if indeed we share in his sufferings in order that we may also share in his glory."*

Chapter 3

The Work of the Holy Spirit in the Life of Jesus Christ

Virgin Birth

Never was it heard, nor will it ever happen again that a virgin woman would become pregnant with a child without union with a man. The prophet Isaiah foretold the virgin birth more than seven hundred years before Jesus was born of the Virgin Mary. *"Therefore the Lord himself shall give you a sign; Behold, a virgin shall conceive, and bear a son, and shall call his name Immanuel"* (Isaiah 7:14).

In Luke 1:34-35 we read the fulfillment of Isaiah's prophecy. *"Then said Mary unto the angel, how shall this be, seeing I know not a man? And the angel answered and said to her, The Holy Ghost will come upon you, and the power of the Highest will overshadow you; therefore, also, that Holy One who is to be born will be called the Son of God."*

As shown in the above scriptural passages, the formation of our Lord's material body was the work of the Holy Spirit. After God created man in His own image, man unfortunately toppled into transgression, and from then on, heaven's mission was redeeming man. Therefore, to redeem man from sin and pay his penalty according to the scheme of redemption, sinless blood was required; without the shedding of blood there is no remission (Hebrews 9:22). Angels were not qualified to do it; they had no blood. The only One qualified to do it was God Himself, and therefore God sent His only begotten Son. He was made and fashioned like the first Adam. However, there is a difference between the two, as expressed by the Apostle Paul in 1 Corinthians 15:45, *"The first man Adam became a living being. The last Adam became a life-giving spirit"(NKJV).*

Jesus Lived a Life Full of the Holy Spirit

Although Christ was conceived of the Holy Spirit, He had to put on a material body similar to ours. He lived, walked, and ate just like us. He was God-Man. John in his gospel presented Him as the Son of God, while Mark presented Him as the son of man (fully God and fully man). As a hundred percent man, He was subjected to similar temptation. The Bible tells us that He was in all points tempted like we are, yet without sin. Remember, the first Adam fell into transgression when he was tempted by the devil, but how did the second Adam do it without failing? He did it through the power of the Holy Spirit. He was full of the Holy Ghost (Luke 4:1).

Before Christ's incarnation, Isaiah had already alluded to the Holy Spirit giving Him wisdom and understanding. *"The Spirit of the LORD shall rest upon Him, The Spirit of wisdom and understanding, The Spirit of counsel and might, The Spirit of knowledge and of the fear of the LORD His delight is in the fear of the LORD, And He shall not judge by the sight of His eyes, Nor decide by the hearing of His ears"* (Isaiah 11:2-3, NKJV). In fact, He was empowered by the Holy Spirit (Acts 10:38; Luke 4:18).

"How God anointed Jesus of Nazareth with the Holy Ghost and with power: who went about doing good, and healing all that were oppressed of the devil; for God was with him" (Acts 10:38). The same Holy Ghost is available to us believers.

Christ's Anointing

The anointing of Christ with the Holy Spirit made Him fitted for His ministry. Jesus the Son of God lived His earthly life victoriously, and I believe one of the reasons He stayed here on earth for thirty-three years was to show us how to be victorious. We cannot live a victorious life apart from the Holy Spirit. Jesus demonstrated it. He quoted it to the hearing of the people. In Luke 4:18, Jesus said, *"The Spirit of the Lord is upon me, because he hath anointed me to preach the gospel to the poor; he hath sent me to heal the brokenhearted, to preach deliverance to the captives, and recovering of sight to the blind, to set at liberty them that are bruised."*

Jesus' Temptation (A Proving Ground)

What we normally call the temptation of Jesus can be viewed as a proving ground. It proved He was the sinless Son of God, capable of redeeming mankind from sin. It may appear strange that the Holy Spirit, who was responsible for the formation of our Lord's body and filling Him with His power, was also responsible for leading Him to the proving ground. After Jesus' baptism in the River Jordan by John the Baptist, we are told, the heavens were opened unto Jesus, and He saw the Spirit of God descending as a dove and lighting upon Him; then a voice from heaven confirmed that He was truly the beloved Son of God, and also that God was well pleased with Him. The next thing we are told is that Jesus was led by the Spirit into the wilderness to be tempted of the devil. His overcoming all these temptations showed He couldn't be subdued like Adam and Eve, or like any of us who could easily succumb to the dictates of the devil.

It is important for you and me not to think that after we are filled with the Holy Spirit, we are free from the trials and temptations of the enemy. In fact, it is something we should be prepared for, and we should pray that we stand and pass the enemy's temptations.

Think about this: as a student, before you can graduate, don't you have to go through tests to prove whether you are fit for the diploma? Having worked in the automotive industry for many years as a product and manufacturing engineer, I'm familiar with proving grounds. When we come up with a new design or model, after it has been manufactured, it must go to a proving ground before it goes on the road. This is to prove what we say the vehicle is capable of. With advancements in technology today, we can do computer simulations for crashworthiness, but going through a true proving ground is still mandatory. We subject the vehicle to a harsh environment to prove its reliability and safety.

Let us carefully take time to study the temptations and perhaps learn how Jesus overcame Satan, so that we can use His method when the enemy tempts us. Satan's strategy has not changed, because it works well for him. He used the same method on Adam and Eve, and he is still doing the same today.

Jesus was led to the wilderness where there was no support: a lonely environment where it might be easy to fall prey to Satan and its demons. I believe Eve easily fell to the temptation of Satan because she was alone; if Adam had been close to her, he probably would have reminded her of what God said concerning that fruit. When believers are together, it will be hard for any of them to commit sins such as fornication or stealing, but if you are alone with the opposite sex and you are not watchful, you can easily fall.

Though Jesus was tempted in this lonely wilderness, He did not fail. The Bible says, *"For we have not an high priest which cannot be touched with the feeling of our infirmities; but was in all points tempted like as we are, yet without sin"* (Hebrews 4:15).

Temptation One:

Satan came to Jesus and said, *"If You are the Son of God, command that these stones become bread."* This was after Jesus had fasted for forty days and forty nights. Fasting for just a day is enough to make one hungry, let alone forty days. Naturally, Jesus was hungry, and Satan, knowing this, came in subtleness to tempt Him with the physical need of the moment: food. First, Satan wanted to cast doubts on His Sonship, saying, "If you are the Son of God." You will notice that God had just declared in Matthew 3:17, *"This is My beloved Son, in whom I am well pleased."* Satan knew He was the Son of God, and Jesus knew whose Son He was. But Satan is a deceiver, a liar, and the father of lies. Hear what Jesus said of him in John 8:44: *"He was a murderer from the beginning, and abode not in the truth, because there is no truth in him. When he speaketh a lie, he speaketh of his own: for he is a liar, and the father of it."* Satan used the same method when he approached Eve in the Garden of Eden, asking, "Has God indeed said, 'You shall not eat of every tree of the garden'?" We must be watchful not to fall into Satan's trap.

What is the Lord's response? *"Man shall not live by bread alone, but by every word that proceeds out of the mouth of God"* (Matthew 4:4). This is a quote from Deuteronomy 8:3. In quoting from this verse, the Lord seems to be referring back to Israel's wilderness experience. The spirit of God led Jesus into the desert for forty days and forty nights in order for Him to go through what Israel had experienced in the wilderness for forty years.

Remember, we are told in Matthew 4:1 that Jesus was full of the Holy Spirit, so He stood His ground by speaking the Word of God, teaching us that when the devil attacks us or tempts us, we must not be silent or passive, but use our weapon, the word of God against him. Ephesians 6:17 tells us to take the helmet of salvation, and the sword of the Spirit, which is the Word of God. And we know the Word of God is quick, and powerful, and sharper than any two-edged sword (Hebrews 4:12).

The plan of Satan was that Jesus would act independently of God the Father as a Son by turning stones into bread, which was not the will of the Father. God provided manna for the children of Israel in the wilderness, and commanded a bird to bring food to Elijah at the brook Cherith. If the Father wanted Jesus to eat then, He would have made the provision. God knows our needs; all we have to do is to call on Him. And remember, God has ordered our steps, He knows the appropriate time, and He will not fail. Don't fall into the tricks of the enemy. When you are in doubt, ask yourself, "Is it in line with the will of God?" and if not, don't do it! But if you don't read or study the Word of God, how will you know?

Temptation Two:

In the second temptation, Satan took Jesus into the holy city, set Him on the pinnacle of the temple, and said to Him, *"If thou be the Son of God, cast thyself down: for it is written, He shall give his angels charge concerning thee: and in their hands they shall bear thee up, lest at any time thou dash thy foot against a stone"* (Matthew 4:6).

It is funny that the devil would imitate Jesus by quoting Scripture in the second temptation. Jesus quoted the Bible in response to the first temptation; Satan wanted to try it too and quoted from Psalm 91:11-12, but omitted an important phrase, "in all Your ways." There is no guarantee for protection unless you follow God's will. In this temptation, Satan wanted Jesus to manipulate God into saving Him from destruction. Satan told Jesus to jump in order to force God into protecting Him. Jesus would put Himself in unnecessary danger. The Bible tells us that God is sovereign, God is in charge, and we are not. We cannot manipulate or control God. God controls us. God is operating all things according to the counsel of His own will (Ephesians 1:11)—not ours. Jesus didn't have to jump to prove

His trust in the Father; He demonstrated it by trusting in God's Word.

Jesus responded by saying, *"It is written again, 'You shall not tempt the LORD your God.'"* (Matthew 4:7; Luke 4:12). This is a quote from Deuteronomy 6:16. Here Satan was appealing to display of popularity.

Many believers test God by putting themselves deliberately in harm's way and expecting God to deliver them from destruction. This is presumptuous sin. Some may be living recklessly, either morally or financially; this is putting God to the test. Remember, whatever seed we sow, there is a harvest. If you are driving your car at 90 mph where you should be going at 60 mph and you are hoping the police do not stop you and write you a ticket, or hoping not to have an accident, that is reckless and manipulative! Or if you say within yourself, "God, give me this or that, and then I will know that You love me," it is equally manipulative. The Bible says, *"Woe unto them that draw iniquity with cords of vanity, and sin as it were with a cart rope: that say, Let him make speed, and hasten his work, that we may see it: and let the counsel of the Holy One of Israel draw nigh and come, that we may know it!"* (Isaiah 5:18-19).

Temptation Three:

In the third temptation, the devil took Jesus up on an exceedingly high mountain, and showed Him all the kingdoms of the world and their glory. And he said to Him, *"All these things I will give You if You will fall down and worship me"* (Matthew 4:8-9; Luke 4:5-6). Satan was now appealing to power or glory. In Luke's account, Satan said, *"For that is delivered unto me; and to whomsoever I will I give it."* He was right about that statement, because Adam handed it over to him freely due to sin. Satan is also known as the *"god of this age"* (2 Corinthians 4:4) and *"the prince of this world"* (John 12:31). He knew ultimately everything would come under Christ, the King of kings and Lord of lords. However, it was not yet time, and it was never going to be handed to Jesus by Satan. Satan wanted to hand over the kingdom right then on his own terms: bow down and worship me. Satan's offer was that Christ would not have to go to the cross and thereby not fulfill the prophecy of Isaiah 53:

"He is despised and rejected of men; a man of sorrows, and acquainted with grief: and we hid as it were our faces from him; he was despised, and we esteemed him not. Surely he hath borne our griefs, and carried our sorrows: yet we did esteem him stricken, smitten of God, and afflicted. But he was wounded for our transgressions, he was bruised for our iniquities: the chastisement of our peace was upon him; and with his stripes we are healed" (Isaiah 53:3-5).

The scheme of man's salvation designed by God the Father, God the Son, and God the Holy Spirit from the beginning would have been thwarted if Christ had yielded to his temptation. But praise be to our Lord and Savior, who replied to the devil, *"Away with you, Satan! For it is written, 'You shall worship the LORD your God, and Him only you shall serve'"* (Matthew 4:10). We must follow the example of our Lord Jesus. Many times we look for instant fixes, which may not be God's plan for us, especially when we think there will be a delay. When Satan comes and offers his plan, because it looks faster, we follow sheepishly. This of course leads to sorrow or downfall. God has a plan for each of us: *"For I know the plans I have for you, declares the LORD, plans to prosper you and not to harm you, plans to give you hope and a future"* (Jeremiah 29:11).

What Can We Learn from the Temptation of Our Lord?

(1) Satan appealed to the physical appetite (Matthew 4:3). This was the exact way he tempted Eve in the Garden of Eden (Genesis 3:1-3). This is to warn us to be careful and watchful along this line, for many fall into sin because of lack of self-

control when it comes to food and especially drinking (wine). The Apostle Paul admonishes that we should be filled with the Spirit rather than drunk on wine, which leads to debauchery (Ephesians 5:18).

(2) Satan followed the first temptation with the desire for personal gain (Matthew 4:6). The way the devil tempted Eve was also similar (Genesis 3:5-6), and many today have fallen into sin because of covetousness, such as chasing after other people's wives and money. The Bible says, *"For the love of money is the root of all evil: which while some coveted after, they have erred from the faith, and pierced themselves through with many sorrows"* (1 Timothy 6:10).

(3) Again, Satan tempted Jesus with an easy way to power or glory (Matthew 4:8-9); in the same fashion he tempted Eve (Genesis 3:5-6). The best way to power is to follow the path of God, which is always enduring or lasting.

Our Lord triumphed over all the temptations of Satan because He depended on the power of the Holy Spirit. If Jesus Christ, the only begotten Son of God, lived and worked upon the power of the Holy Spirit, how much more should we depend on Him in every step of our life, in every stage of our service, and when we are faced with Satan and sin? Jesus used the Word of God every time Satan tried to get Him to deviate from the path of truth. This Word is at our disposal, it works on Satan, and we will overcome him by the Word. The Word is our strong weapon.

In order to triumph like our Lord, we must walk in His pathway. In 1 John 2:6, we read, *"He who says he abides in Him ought himself also to walk just as He walked."* Jesus depended entirely on the Holy Spirit and on the Word of God.

Miracles

Jesus Christ wrought His miracles here on earth by the power of the Holy Spirit. In Matthew 12:28, we read, *"But if I cast out demons by the Spirit of God, surely the kingdom of God has come upon you."* It is through the Spirit that miracle-working power has been given to some in the church after our Lord's departure from this earth. *"By the same Spirit, to another gifts of healings by the same Spirit, to another the working of miracles"* (1 Corinthians 12:9-10).

His Resurrection

Just as they were in the creation, God the Father, God the Son, and God the Holy Spirit were all involved in the triumphant resurrection of Jesus Christ. When the Father saw that the sinless blood of Jesus had been offered, justice was satisfied. The penalty for man's sin had been paid in full. Nothing more was required by God's law. He ordered Him to be loosed. *"He raised him from the dead, and set him at his own right hand in the heavenly places"* (Ephesians 1:20).

Jesus Christ through His own power and majesty rose from death. The grave has no power over Him. Jesus said, *"I laid down my life, that I might take it again"* (John 10:17).

The power of the Holy Spirit was equally involved in raising Jesus Christ from the dead. We see this in 1 Peter 3:18, *"For Christ also hath once suffered for sins, the just for the unjust, that he might bring us to God, being put to death in the flesh, but quickened by the Spirit."*

Also, Romans 1:4 tells us, *"Through the Spirit of holiness was declared with power to be the Son of God by his resurrection from the dead: Jesus Christ our Lord."* We also read in Romans 8:11, *"But if the*

Spirit of him that raised up Jesus from the dead dwell in you, he that raised up Christ from the dead shall also quicken your mortal bodies by his Spirit that dwelleth in you."

Chapter 4

Another Comforter

"But the Comforter [Counselor, Helper, Intercessor, Advocate, Strengthener, Standby], the Holy Spirit, Whom the Father will send in My name [in My place, to represent Me and act on My behalf], He will teach you all things. And He will cause you to recall [will remind you of, bring to your remembrance] everything I have told you" (John 14:26, Amplified).

"But when the Comforter is come, whom I will send unto you from the Father, even the Spirit of truth, which proceedeth from the Father, he shall testify of me" (John 15:26).

"Nevertheless I tell you the truth; It is expedient for you that I go away: for if I go not away, the Comforter will not come unto you; but if I depart, I will send him unto you" (John 16:7).

The above passages are part of the Upper Room discourse before Jesus had to go to the cross. Jesus had spent over three years with His disciples; He comforted them, taught them, and met their needs. When they were faced with a storm and were afraid, they cried unto Him, and He calmed the storm and alleviated their fears. When they needed to pay taxes, they looked unto Him. Now that it was time for Him to leave them physically, He assured them of another Comforter who would represent Him. Jesus said it was expedient for them that He went away: that is to say, it was to their advantage, or for their good, because if He did not go, the Comforter would not come.

Why was it to their advantage? The Comforter would be with them forever, and live within them and in every believer. He would remind them of what Jesus had taught. He still guides us into all truth, and counsels and helps us. These words must have been comforting to the disciples then, and still are to us today.

When we look closely at the Greek word *parakletos*, translated as "Comforter" and referring to the Holy Spirit, the root word has other meanings. It could mean advocate, teacher, counselor, intercessor, or helper.

Advocate

What is the work of an advocate? An advocate is by your side to aid you in a case, to speak on your behalf. When you are summoned to court before a judge, you need an advocate or a lawyer who understands the law and knows how to defend or plead your case, or else you might go to jail or pay a heavy fine. Believers' archenemy is Satan, who accuses us day and night before God.

"And I heard a loud voice saying in heaven, Now is come salvation, and strength, and the kingdom of our God, and the power of his Christ: for the accuser of our brethren is cast down, which accused them before our God day and night" (Revelation 12:10). The Holy Spirit is our advocate on this earth, pleading against our enemy Satan and his agents. And again, see how blessed we are, because Jesus the Author and Finisher of our faith is sitting at the right hand of the throne of God (Hebrews 12:2; Colossians 3:1).

How were Peter and John able to plead before the council fearlessly and confess our Lord Jesus? They said to them, "You judge whether it is right in God's sight to obey you rather than God." You can also see how Paul pleaded before King Agrippa adeptly in Acts 26. How were they able to do it? The Holy Spirit, the Advocate; it was certainly not these men, but the Holy Spirit pleading through them.

One of the lessons my wife and I learned in our early days in the United States is that you cannot legally discipline your child any way you like. We had a big problem with the law when we thought we had disciplined one of our kids who was wayward. It got to the police, and when they came, we opened up and went as far as saying we flogged the child, not knowing flogging was not a word for discipline but regarded as child abuse. It became a big case to the extent of going before a judge. Despite being students with limited financial resources, we had to hire an attorney. The case dragged on for a while until we had no money to pay the lawyer. We then decided to go on our own with prayer. To our amazement, the first time without a lawyer was the day we were set free. The Holy Spirit advocated through us and for us, and favor came. The Lord Jesus said, *"The Holy Spirit shall teach you in the same hour what you ought to say"* (Luke 12:12).

Another way the Holy Spirit advocates is in the hearts of men. The Holy Spirit begins to plead in stubborn hearts that have rejected the teaching of the Word of God. With the pleading of the Holy Spirit, their hearts are illumined and they surrender to God. We ministers do not know the best words to use to get the job done, but the Holy Spirit advocates with great success through us and over the stubbornness in the hearts of people.

Counselor

A counselor is a person who studies a situation and gives advice or recommends a course of action. In the Old Testament, kings used counselors, and these were wise men who had insight (1 Chronicles 27:32). The Holy Spirit, who is all-wise and sees all things past, present, and future, is the One who will represent Jesus as He goes back to His Father in heaven. And He will be with the disciples and all believers always.

Almost every church organization and many organizations in the secular world have counselors to help individuals deal with certain problems. They could be in the area of drug abuse, drinking, smoking, pornography, or even marital problems. Many of these counselors are good and wonderful; they have helped countless people. However, the lasting solution is to get the Holy Spirit involved. I have heard and talked with people, even Christians, who have struggled with diverse habits and behaviors that they would like to change, but somehow can't seem to. They know these addictions are both destructive and sinful. Many have gone to pastors, counselors, or even rehabilitation centers, but as soon as they get out of the program they go back to the same behavior. It is reported that hotels make a lot of money from adult movies (sexual immorality) when they host Christian conferences. It is not new that even ministers of the gospel are caught in these behaviors.

Many have become frustrated with the possibility of change and wonder if they should stop going to counseling. There are many good books out there on how to change destructive habits, and pastors, counselors, and Christian psychologists work vehemently to help people, yet some people still do not have a lasting solution. Why? Perhaps we have misunderstood the role we play in change as well as the role the Holy Spirit plays in helping someone break an addiction by His counsel. Hear Paul's prayer for the believers in Ephesians 3:16: *"That He would grant you, according to the riches of His glory, to be strengthened with might through His Spirit in the inner man."* The Holy Spirit is the great Counselor who strengthens God's people in the inner man to overcome any addiction. When we do our part in teaching and counseling, we need to introduce people to the Third Person of the Godhead, who is the Holy Spirit, the mighty Counselor. He strengthens from the inside out.

There is a chorus that goes thus:

Someone on the inside working on the outside,
Oh, what a change in my life,
Oh, what a miracle change in my life.

Teacher

Who is better to teach you all things than the Author of the Book? Peter stated that the prophecy never came by the will of man, but holy men of God spoke *as they were* moved by the Holy Spirit (2 Peter 1:21).

Have you ever wondered how some people of God who have never been inside the four walls of a classroom become excellent teachers of the Word of God? In my early years, the elders who taught us never had the privilege of going to school. In fact, some of them could hardly read, but they taught the Word flawlessly. How? By the Holy Spirit! The man whom God used to reach the heart of Charles Spurgeon, who eventually became a great preacher, was said to be an illiterate.

If we replace "comforter" with "teacher" in John 14:26, it reads: *"And I will pray the Father, and he shall give you another Teacher, that he may abide with you forever. But the Teacher, which is the Holy Spirit, whom the Father will send in my name, he shall teach you all things, and bring all things to your remembrance, whatsoever I have said unto you."*

Hear what the so-called religious leaders of the temple, the priests, the captain of the temple, and the Sadducees said concerning the disciples of Jesus Christ after they had been filled with the Holy Spirit: *"Now when they saw the boldness of Peter and John, and perceived that they were unlearned and ignorant men, they marveled; and they took knowledge of them, that they had been with Jesus"* (Acts 4:13). They had been taught by our Lord Jesus. He was their Rabbi, their good Teacher. But now they were taught by the Holy Spirit who lived in them. These highly educated people could not fathom the great things that were done through the disciples by the Holy Spirit.

I believe you must have experienced reading a portion of the Bible several times and even listening to lectures or sermons by men about it without quite grasping it. Then, suddenly, a light shines in your spirit and gives you an unmatched understanding, and you wonder why you did not understand it before. So what happened? The Holy Spirit illumined your heart and opened your understanding, and here comes the revelation. Glory to God!

This Divine Teacher will not only teach us all things, but will bring to our remembrance all things. You may have had this promise come to pass in your own life, where the Holy Spirit suddenly brought a Scripture to your mind that met your need at that moment: it could be safety from a car accident, or a specific message the Holy Spirit wanted to speak to His people.

I can remember an instance when a fellow minister told me, without prior notice, to bring a message for the people. In such a situation, you ask the Holy Spirit to help you bring what the congregation needs, not what you know in your head or some sermon you preached recently. Immediately the Holy Spirit brought into my spirit what I should preach and reminded me of the verses that I did not write down. After I preached, the minister showed me the note he was going to use, and it was identical to what I preached unprepared.

Note again what Jesus said in this verse: *"He will bring to your remembrance what he had said."* What Jesus said is what is written in His Word—the Bible. If you don't study your Bible, how are you going to know what He has said or what the Holy Spirit will remind you of? Therefore, it is imperative that we study His Word.

Comforter

The Holy Spirit, who is omniscient and the all-wise God, is the best to comfort us in our sorrow. He knows the root cause of our sorrow. Nothing is hidden before Him, so He knows the right words to use. Job's friends wanted to comfort him in his peril, but instead of comforting Him, they added to his miseries because they had no knowledge of the root cause. Job referred to them as *"miserable comforters"* (Job 16:2).

The Holy Spirit has continued to be my loving and faithful Comforter since my wife departed this world about three years ago. I do not know how any human being can comfort me in this sorrowful situation. My wife and I were dear friends. We were married for thirty-seven years, understood each other very well, and had dreams and plans of what we wanted to do together for the rest of our lives. We were looking forward to our children's weddings and more grandchildren, believing and confessing Psalm 91:16. But suddenly she went home to be with the Lord. I was devastated. Family and friends tried to comfort me and ease my broken heart, but the moment they left, uneasiness and discomfort would start all over again. The Holy Spirit, who abides in and with me, continues His divine counsel and comfort. No human being can do it, and no amount of human words or gifts will suffice: only the Holy Spirit.

Several months before my wife's departure, the Lord had me study more on the Holy Spirit. I did not know what was coming, but God is all-knowing. He knows about our needs and how to prepare us. A few days before her death, I mistakenly turned my *Daily Bread* to February 8, 2013, instead of January 8, 2013, and she departed on January 18. The summary page for that day was as follows:

> "Precious in the sight of the LORD is the death of His saints."—Psalm 116:15
>
> "Sometimes when the infinite God conveys His thoughts to finite man, mystery is the result. For example, there's a profound verse in the book of Psalms that seems to present more questions than answers: "Precious in the sight of the LORD is the death of His faithful servants" (116:15 NIV).
>
> I shake my head and wonder how that can be. I see things with earthbound eyes, and I have a tough time seeing what is "precious" about the fact that our daughter was taken in a car accident at the age of 17—or that any of us have lost cherished loved ones.
>
> We begin to unwrap the mystery, though, when we consider that what is precious to the Lord is not confined to earthly blessings. This verse examines a heaven-based perspective. For instance, I know from Psalm 139:16 that Melissa's arrival in God's heaven was expected. God was looking for her arrival and it was precious in His eyes. And think about this: Imagine the Father's joy when He welcomes His children home and sees their absolute ecstasy in being face to face with His Son (see John 17:24). When death comes for the follower of Christ, God opens His arms to welcome that person into His presence. Even through our

tears, we can see how precious that is in God's eyes.

Lord, when sorrow grips our hearts as we think about the death of one close to us, remind us of the joy You are experiencing as our loved one enjoys the pleasures of heaven. Please allow that to give us hope and comfort."

"A sunset in one land is a sunrise in another."

As I was reading, fear came upon me, but at this time no one knew she would die of her illness. After I discovered it was a wrong date, I quickly closed the page and began to confess Psalm 91:16, *"With long life will I satisfy him, and shew him my salvation."* I believe the Spirit was revealing to me what was coming, but no one wants to hear that. Since I was then in a period of prayer and fasting, I continued to intensify my prayer, but the Giver of life knows when our time will be over down here.

She had been a woman of strength and of great faith. For most of her life she had never been held back by any serious sickness or illness. There was a day when she had a painful backache, and she was scheduled to work. I told her to call off, but she said she wouldn't like to disappoint the lady she was going to work for and refused to go to the hospital. She promised me that if God didn't take the pain away by the following day, she would go to the hospital. She requested that I drop her at work; I reluctantly dropped her off after we prayed. Miraculously, before morning, the pain had completely gone. We believe in divine healing, though we don't reject going to see a doctor if one is sick.

Her blood pressure was almost perfect at any time of the day (120/80). She had extraordinary strength. She would sometimes mow the grass and shovel snow without problems. This probably contributed to her not going for checkups that would have detected the growth in her rectum that eventually became a cancerous tumor. Death is, of course, a vehicle that takes believers to heaven whichever way it comes. She is resting in the bosom of Jesus Christ, seeing Father Abraham.

You too may be experiencing sorrow. The only One who remains our loving, faithful, and all-wise Comforter is the Holy Spirit. And He lives in you if you are a believer; lean on Him.

Intercessor

An intercessor intervenes on behalf of another; he can intervene without the knowledge of the one needing help. The Holy Spirit as our Intercessor goes on our behalf to the Father without us necessarily knowing. As our Helper, He assists us in our efforts when we are weak and unable to do it alone. But as our Intercessor, He goes on our behalf to intervene whether we are aware of the need or not, and whether we pray for it or not, because He knows we need it.

As believers, we have the great privilege of approaching the throne of God (grace) with our prayers. This accessibility is of course through our Lord Jesus Christ, who made the sacrifice with His life and brought peace between us and God. The book of Hebrews tells us that we should come boldly to the throne of grace, that we may obtain mercy and find grace to help in time of need (Hebrews 4:16).

Then why do we need an intercessor or someone to intervene on our behalf? The answer is what we find in Romans 8:26: *"Likewise the Spirit also helps in our weaknesses. For we do not know what we should pray for as we ought, but the Spirit Himself makes intercession for us with groanings which cannot be uttered."*

We Do Not Know How to Pray as We Should:

Many times we think we know what we need, but we do not ask for things that are necessary for all things to work together for our good and according to His purpose. Why? Because we do not know. For example, if a child is not guided and given a balanced diet, all he asks for are sugary things, because it is pleasurable to his taste buds. However, the wise mother mixes his food with other things like vegetables or fruits that will give him a healthy body. The Holy Spirit intercedes on our behalf because He knows exactly what we need for our spiritual vitality.

While Jesus was physically on earth, He operated fully as a man. Listen to His prayer when He raised Lazarus from the dead, *"I know that You always hear Me"* (John 11:42). Why were His prayers always heard? Because He always asked according to the will of God; He knew the will of God. The Apostle John tells us in 1 John 5:14-15, *"Now this is the confidence that we have in Him, that if we ask anything according to His will, He hears us. And if we know that He hears us, whatever we ask, we know that we have the petitions that we have asked of Him."* That is why we need the help of an Intercessor who is conversant with the will of the Father.

We Don't Always Know the Mind of God:

No matter how close we are to God, we only know whatever He reveals to us. Deuteronomy 29:29 says, *"The secret things belong unto the LORD our God: but those things which are revealed belong unto us and to our children for ever, that we may do all the words of this law."* But the Holy Spirit knows the mind of God. He knows His plans for us and He knows the steps we are to take to reach our destiny. The journey to reach our destination sometimes may appear too long, and we may want to take shortcuts, which may not be the best for us.

In the parable of the tares, the enemy (Satan) came and sowed tares with the good seed in the field. The servants wanted to immediately uproot the tares, but the master told them to let them both grow together until harvest. There are some things in our lives that we may want to uproot right away, but the Holy Spirit knows best when and how to uproot them without causing us any harm. We surely need the Holy Spirit to be our Intercessor. Fortunately, we also have our Lord Jesus, who is at the right hand of God making intercession for us (Romans 8:34; Hebrews 7:25).

Believers Are to Be Intercessors for Others:

In both the Old and New Testaments, people of God interceded for others and saved many lives. In fact, God is looking to us to become intercessors for others. In Ezekiel 22:30, God said, *"And I sought for a man among them that should make up the hedge, and stand in the gap before me for the land, that I should not destroy it: but I found none."*

Abraham interceded for Sodom time and time again (Genesis 18). Moses interceded for the children of Israel (Exodus 32:11-13; 31-32). Nehemiah also prayed, interceding for his people (Nehemiah 1:3-11). The greatest intercessor is, of course, our Lord Jesus, who interceded for believers before going to the Father (John 17:6-26). Stephen was another intercessor who prayed for his murderers at the point of his death; his prayer, I believe, helped in turning things around for Saul who became Paul, who was greatly used by God to propagate the gospel. The same Paul urged believers to intercede for all people. We read in 1 Timothy 2:1-3, *"I exhort therefore, that, first of all, supplications, prayers, intercessions, and giving of thanks, be made for all men; For kings, and for all that are in authority; that we may lead a quiet and peaceable life in all godliness and honesty. For this is good and acceptable in the sight of God our Savior."*

Helper

A helper is someone who assists you or gives you support in achieving your endeavors or completing your assignments. When you have an assignment that may be too much for you, you need a helper. The helper not only assists you in completing your work, but serves as an encourager or inspirer to continue the work. When God saw that Adam was alone and needed a helper, He created Eve to supply what he lacked. Marriage is not only for reproduction, but for companionship and help. Eve was there to help him physically, emotionally, and in other aspects of life. Adam named everything that God created; that is a lot of work. I believe Eve would have encouraged him and handed him water and food.

Who needs help? I believe the simple answer is everyone. However, to get appropriate help, you must be doing something. Of course, if you are doing nothing, you need some kind of help; you can't be lazy and expect things to go well. This is to say the Holy Spirit is our Helper; we must pray the way we know how to. The Scriptures say the Holy Spirit helps in our infirmities—that is, in our lack of strength or capability and not knowing how to pray as we should.

His work is to assist us. That means we don't just sit around doing nothing or simply wait on Him to do it all. We must do our part; we must pray the way we know how. He assists with our effort to get it right. You do your part and He carries it and aligns your prayer with the will of the Father.

You don't get the proper help until you do something. I remember in college, I wanted to earn an A in technical writing. People who had taken that course said the professor was tough and it would be very hard to get a good grade. But I asked myself, "Why can't I have the grade I desire?" I was determined to work hard. A giant part of what determined the final grade was the weekly papers we had to write. In the first paper, I went to ask the professor a question, and he asked me to go and read his instructions. I then determined to always go to him with a draft. Within three days of the assignment, my draft was ready and I would take it to him; he would look the paper over and make comments. I carefully followed his remarks and wrote it the way he wanted. At the end of the semester, I got the grade I desired. Without going to him with a draft (doing something), I would not have had the proper help I needed to get the grade I desired. For us to receive the appropriate or proper help, we must do our part, while the Holy Spirit does His.

Having the Holy Spirit as your helper gives you numerous advantages. For example, (1) the Holy Spirit has your accurate information, (2) the Holy Spirit is always available, and (3) the Holy Spirit understands your language or dialect.

The Holy Spirit Has Your Accurate Information:

The Holy Spirit is omniscient. He knows your past and future. He knows the right balm to apply to your wound. If you go to a doctor to seek help for your sickness, you will be asked to fill out a long and boring form about your medical history before they can help you. The Holy Spirit knows both your history and your future; He knows the root cause of your problems, and He will align your prayer with the will of the Father. That is why the Scriptures say there is nothing too hard for God. *"Ah Lord GOD! behold, thou hast made the heaven and the earth by thy great power and stretched out arm, and there is nothing too hard for thee"* (Jeremiah 32:17).

The Holy Spirit Is Always Available:

The Holy Spirit is available to help us 24/7, and there is no waiting line. Even with advancements in technology where we have the Internet and helplines, these are human sources of help and are limited. No human solution can be compared to a divine one. Jesus says He will abide with us forever. And in Hebrews 13:5-6 we are told, *"I will never leave you nor forsake you."* So we may boldly say: *"The LORD is my helper; I will not fear. What can man do to me?"*

The Holy Spirit Understands Your Language or Dialect:

There is no communication barrier. There is no language or dialect the Holy Spirit does not understand; He created them. You do not have to speak in Hebrew or Greek for Him to help you. If you are seeking help from people, sometimes they might tell you they cannot understand you, and as such they cannot give you the needed help. But with the Holy Spirit, you can speak in your mother tongue, or if you speak in unknown tongues, that is equally good.

Chapter 5

Baptism with the Holy Spirit

"I indeed baptize you with water unto repentance: but he that cometh after me is mightier than I, whose shoes I am not worthy to bear: he shall baptize you with the Holy Ghost, and with fire" (Matthew 3:11).

The expression "baptism with the Holy Spirit" is a derivative of "baptize with the Holy Spirit," first spoken by John the Baptist. It appears in all four Gospels and also the Book of Acts (Matthew 3:11; Mark 1:8; Luke 3:16; John 1:33; Acts 1:5, 11:6). John made the statement while he was baptizing at the River Jordan. He saw many of the Pharisees and Sadducees coming for his baptism, and wondered who had warned them to flee from the wrath of God upon the unrepentant. These groups of people were the self-proclaimed pious men of his day, but had no place in their hearts for God. Jesus called them hypocrites. However, when they heard John's preaching, many of them came to him to be baptized. Water baptism normally follows repentance—that is, saying publicly, "I'm now totally for Christ."

John the Gospel-writer, in his record, reports that the Jews sent priests and Levites to John the Baptist to ask him whether he was Christ (the long-awaited Messiah), Elias, or that prophet, but he plainly told them he was only *"the voice of one crying in the wilderness, Make straight the way of the Lord"* (Isaiah 40:3; John 1:23). They further pressed John to reveal who he was, because they could not understand why he was baptizing if he was not Christ. He told them that all he was capable of doing was to baptize with water, but there was One coming after him who would baptize them with the Holy Spirit. And John began to describe the superiority of the One coming after him, who was actually before him, and whose shoe's latchet he was not worthy to untie.

Again, John the Baptist gave the main reason why he was baptizing in John 1:31: *"And I knew him not: but that he should be made manifest to Israel, therefore am I come baptizing with water."* Please look at this verse closely. John said he did not know that Christ was the One God sent who was preferred before him; John was quite right about that. You might wonder why John said he did not know Him—after all, they were related. Remember, when the angel appeared to Mary concerning the conception of Christ through the Holy Spirit, the angel also told her that her cousin Elisabeth was pregnant in her old age. That pregnancy was John the Baptist, so he and Jesus probably played together while growing up. Of course, John might have noticed something special about Jesus, but at this point in time he did not know He was the Redeemer that Israel had been waiting for. It is God, through the Holy Spirit, that reveals to us who Christ is. When Jesus asked His disciples, *"'But who do you say that I am?' Simon Peter answered and said, 'You are the Christ, the Son of the living God.' Jesus answered and said to him, 'Blessed are you, Simon Bar-Jonah, for flesh and blood has not revealed this to you, but My Father who is in heaven'"* (Matthew 16:16-17, NKJV).

The second thing I want us to notice is in the last part of the verse: *"But that He should be made manifest to Israel, therefore am I come baptizing with water."* John tells us here that since Israel did not know their Messiah was already in their midst, God sent him to baptize with water in order to reveal that to them. John in essence was saying to them, "Your Deliverer is already here. Your King is here! The Prince of Peace, your Immanuel, the One that the prophets had predicted (Isaiah 9:6-7, 7:14; Micah 5:2) is already in your midst!"

Here we see again that the goodness of God is incomprehensible! He will never leave us in darkness. So John bore witness, saying, *"I saw the Spirit descending from heaven like a dove, and He remained upon Him. I did not know Him, but He who sent me to baptize with water said to me, 'Upon whom you see the Spirit descending, and remaining on Him, this is He who baptizes with the Holy Spirit.' And I have seen and testified that this is the Son of God"* (John 1:32-34, NKJV).

What Is Baptism with the Holy Spirit?

Baptism with the Holy Spirit is the heavenly gift from the Father that bestows power on a believer for effective witness and service. The word "baptize" (*baptizo* in Greek) means "to be totally immersed"; to be baptized with the Holy Spirit is to be soaked in the Holy Spirit's life and power. It is the work of the Holy Spirit, separate and distinct from the rebirth or regeneration that occurs when a sinner comes to God with a penitent heart. The experience empowers a believer to carry out his or her assignment from God. It can be compared to grace: John Bevere defines grace as empowerment from God. Following his definition, we can equally say, "Baptism with the Holy Spirit is a heavenly gift from the Father that bestows grace on a believer for effective witness and service." In ourselves we are not capable, but His grace or empowerment enables us to do it. Jesus said, "Without Me you can do nothing."

Baptism with the Holy Spirit was of paramount importance to the early church. They knew the experience was the enduement of power to carry out our Lord's assignment effectively and to do what Jesus did while He walked the earth. No wonder miracles such as healings were prevalent wherever they went. Is that possible today? Yes! Why? Because Jesus is the same, God the Father is the same, and the Holy Spirit is the same: they cannot change. It is the church that needs to align herself with the Holy Spirit so that He can manifest Himself through us.

When the early apostles who were at Jerusalem heard that Samaria had received the Word of God; they immediately sent Peter and John to them, because the Holy Spirit had not yet fallen on them. And when they got there, what did they do? They prayed and laid hands on them, and they received the Holy Spirit. Similarly, when the Apostle Paul got to Ephesus, his question to the believers there was, "Have you received the Holy Spirit since you believed?" And when they told him they had not even heard there was a Holy Spirit, Paul laid hands on them, and immediately the Holy Spirit came on them, and they spoke in tongues and prophesied.

Some Designations Used in the Bible for Baptism with the Holy Spirit

Several terms are found in the Bible, especially in the book of Acts, that are equivalent to the expression "baptize with the Holy Spirit," first spoken by John the Baptist. In Acts 1:5, Jesus said, *"You shall be baptized with the Holy Spirit not many days from now."* Peter echoed the Lord's statement in Acts 11:16. Acts 2:4 used the term *"they were all filled with the Holy Spirit"* on the day of Pentecost. Acts 1:4 calls it "the promise of the Father" (see also Luke 24:29). Acts 1:8, *"the Holy Spirit has come upon you."* Acts 10:44, *"the Holy Spirit fell or fallen upon them"* (see also Acts 8:16, 11:15, 19:6; Luke 1:35, 3:22). Acts 2:38, *"the gift of the Holy Spirit"* (see also Acts 10:45, 11:17). Acts 8:20, *"the gift of God"* (Acts 11:17, 15:8). And *"receiving the Holy Spirit"* (Acts 8:15-19, 19:2).

Water Baptism versus Holy Spirit Baptism

Baptism with the Holy Spirit has been a controversial topic in pneumatology. Bible scholars differ in their interpretation of "baptize you with the Holy Spirit." Some have argued that water baptism is the same thing as baptism with the Holy Spirit. There are those who say the baptism John was talking about (Matthew 3:11), echoed by our Lord (Acts 1:4), is what Paul explained in 1 Corinthians 12:14. And yet there are those who say that the signs such as speaking in tongues that followed the reception of the baptism with the Holy Spirit are no longer for our time.

Please, let us carefully follow what the Bible teaches about the baptism with the Holy Spirit. The Bible is always good at interpreting itself; our God is not an author of confusion. Scripture gives us several clear reasons to believe that baptism with the Holy Spirit is an experience beyond regeneration or water baptism.

First and foremost, if water baptism is the same as baptism with the Holy Spirit, John the Baptist would probably have said, "The One coming after me will continue to water baptize you," or even "He will baptize more people than me." He didn't say that. Instead, he plainly said, *"I baptize you with water, but He shall baptize you with the Holy Spirit."* Remember, John was a prophet. Hear how Jesus described him: *"For I say unto you, among those that are born of women there is not a greater prophet than John the Baptist"* (Luke 7:28). John described Jesus as the One greater than he, whose shoes he was not worthy to untie, the One qualified to baptize with the Holy Spirit. John was the messenger sent by God to prepare the way for the Lord Jesus (Malachi 3:1). He came and preached repentance, and those who came with penitent hearts were given water baptism as a sign that they were now for God. The baptism with the Holy Spirit that Christ gives is for believers, and it is something beyond the water baptism that John was giving.

Our Lord's statement in Acts 1:5 is another reason to believe that baptism in the Holy Spirit is an additional experience beyond water baptism. Jesus said, *"For John truly baptized with water, but you shall be baptized with the Holy Spirit not many days from now."* This statement came forty days after our

Lord had gone to Calvary, died, and been resurrected, thereby completing the work of our redemption. And whom was Jesus addressing here? His disciples and kin followers. These people had followed Him for over three years; they had been taught by the Lord. They were redeemed. Jesus said concerning them in John 17:12, *"While I was with them in the world, I kept them in Your name. Those whom You gave Me I have kept; and none of them is lost except the son of perdition, that the Scripture might be fulfilled."* The only one lost was Judas Iscariot, who betrayed Jesus. Jesus had given these people power to go to the Jews and preach that the kingdom of heaven was at hand, and to heal the sick, cleanse the lepers, raise the dead, and cast out devils. They came back rejoicing and telling Jesus that the demons were subject to them through His name, and Jesus told them they should rejoice because their names were written in heaven. That tells us that they were believers. If baptism in the Holy Spirit is not another experience beyond regeneration or water baptism, why would Jesus ask them to wait until they were baptized with the Holy Spirit? This is another piece of proof that water baptism is not the same as baptism with the Holy Spirit.

Again, we read in Luke 24:49, *"Behold, I send the Promise of My Father upon you; but tarry in the city of Jerusalem until you are endued with power from on high."* Here Jesus speaks to His disciples before his accession. Let us pay close attention to the word "promise" in our Lord's statement. What is the promise of the Father? The Apostle Peter gives us the answer to this question. He said to the people, *"Therefore being exalted to the right hand of God, and having received from the Father the promise of the Holy Spirit, He poured out this which you now see and hear"* (Acts 2:33). The promise of the Father is the pouring out of the Holy Spirit, which is the same as baptism with the Holy Spirit. The prophet Joel foretold the outpouring of the Holy Spirit in chapter two of his book. The promise of the Father is undoubtedly for His children. Every good parent wants to give or leave something good for their children. Jesus puts it this way in Luke 11:13: *"If ye then, being evil, know how to give good gifts unto your children: how much more shall your heavenly Father give the Holy Spirit to them that ask him?"* The promise of the outpouring of the Holy Spirit is for the children, those who are born again; therefore, it is an experience beyond water baptism.

In Acts 8, we read an account of believers in Samaria who were water baptized but had not received the baptism of the Holy Spirit. When Peter and John came to them, they prayed and laid hands on them, and they received the Holy Spirit. A similar account is given in Acts 19 concerning believers in Ephesus who had not been baptized with the Holy Spirit. When the Apostle Paul came to them he simply asked them, "Have you received the Holy Spirit since you believed?" And they answered, "We have not so much as heard whether there is a Holy Spirit." Paul laid his hands upon them, and they received the Holy Spirit and spoke with tongues and prophesied. This is more proof that baptism with the Holy Spirit is not the same as water baptism.

Some have also interpreted baptism with the Holy Spirit as what Paul explained in 1 Corinthians 12:13, *"For by one Spirit are we all baptized into one body, whether we be Jews or Gentiles, whether we be bond or free; and have been all made to drink into one Spirit."* If you follow carefully the whole context in which Paul stated that "we are baptized into one body," you will realize that he was saying that the Holy Spirit is the instrumentation by which the baptizing takes place. It is the work of the Holy Spirit to incorporate every believer into the body of Christ. Christ is the head and we (the church) are the body. We also see equivalent expressions in Romans 6:3, *"were baptized into Christ Jesus,"* and in Galatians 3:27, *"baptized into Christ."* In Ephesians 4:4-5, Paul teaches our oneness in Christ as believers. When anyone comes to Christ, he or she is baptized or incorporated into the body of Christ. Therefore, baptism with the Holy Spirit is a distinct experience from water baptism, and Christ is the One that baptizes in the Holy Spirit.

The Effect of Baptism on Evangelism

After the day of Pentecost, when the apostles and other believers received the baptism with the Holy Spirit, there were great demonstrations of the power through them. They had unmatched boldness to witness Christ, and many were converted, with miracles following wherever they went. In Acts 2:41 after Peter preached, we are told that on the same day, about three thousand souls were added to the church. We also see the miracle of the lame man walking at the gate of the temple called Beautiful (Acts 3:1-9). It wasn't just the apostles, but other believers. For example, Stephen, who was a deacon, full of faith and power, did great wonders and miracles among the people (Acts 6:8). So also was Deacon Philip, who went down to the city of Samaria and preached Christ to them. The result was: *"Multitudes with one accord heeded the things spoken by Philip, hearing and seeing the miracles which he did. For unclean spirits, crying with a loud voice came out of many who were possessed; and many who were paralyzed and lame were healed. And there was great joy in that city"* (Acts 8:5-8). We also read about a demonstration of the power of the Holy Spirit after Philip explained the Word of God to the Ethiopian eunuch; Philip was miraculously transported and the eunuch saw Philip no more.

Demonstrations of the power of the Holy Spirit did not stop with the first-century believers. His signs and wonders are mightily with us, even today. There have been great men of God, some who are resting in the bosom of Jesus Christ, such as John G. Lakes, Smith Wigglesworth, Rev. Kenneth E. Hagins, Oral Roberts, and many others.

You Have to Accept the Promise

Now, if you are a believer you have the right to God's promise—the Holy Spirit. However, you need to accept it. Jesus said in Luke 11:13 *"If you then, being evil, know how to give good gifts to your children, how much more will your heavenly Father give the Holy Spirit to those who ask Him!"* Remember the parable of the prodigal son: as soon as his father saw him, he ran to him and threw his arms around him and kissed him, then began to celebrate his son's return; though he left in disobedience, he came home in repentance.

Now, let us focus on the elder brother. When he came home and saw everyone rejoicing and celebrating that his brother had returned, he was angry, sad, and dejected to the extent that he refused to go in. His father had to plead with him. And he would not refer to the prodigal son as "brother," but as "this son." He told his father that he had always been obedient and the father had not given him even a young goat so that he could celebrate with his friends. But hear what the father said: "All that I have is yours." What God has is ours, but we must accept it. The elder brother missed or did not accept his blessing due to ignorance—he did not enjoy what his father had, which invariably belonged to him.

Unfortunately, many believers today miss out on the promise of the Father, which belongs to all of us. The gift of our heavenly Father, baptism with the Holy Spirit, cannot run out. As He gave to the believers of old, He does the same today. Since time immemorial, earthly fathers have not stopped giving or leaving gifts for their children. Why would the Everlasting Father (El-Shaddai), the All-Sufficient One, the God that is more than enough, stop giving the good gift of the Holy Spirit to His children?

Receiving Baptism with the Holy Spirit and Holiness

Do you receive the baptism with the Holy Spirit because you are holy? No! It is a gift, not an award based on your merits. And the good news is that it is available to all believers. Does receiving the baptism of the Holy Spirit make you holier? It should lead you to holiness, but this is not automatic. Holiness is the nature and character of God produced in believers, which sets you free from spiritual decay. It is a separation from all unholy things and sinful habits (2 Corinthians 7:1). It is attainable and retainable by feeding on the Word of God, just like maturity in the things of God. The Apostle Peter said, *"Like newborn babies, we should desire the sincere milk of the word, so that we may grow thereby"* (1 Peter 2:2). He also urged us to be holy as our God is holy (1 Peter 1:15-16 cf. Lev 11:44-45).

Necessity of Baptism with the Holy Spirit

The necessity of baptism with the Holy Spirit can be seen in its purpose. What is the purpose? Its primary purpose is to empower believers to effectively witness for Christ, not just in the pulpit or Sunday school, but wherever they are called in life. If you are a salesman or a mechanic, you are still an ambassador for Christ, and you need to show it by your words and deeds wherever you work.

Before Christ ascended to His heavenly Father, having finished the work of our redemption, He gave what is usually termed "the Great Commission" to His disciples, *"Go ye into all the world, and preach the gospel to every creature"* (Mark 16:15; Matthew 28:19). Our Lord is conversant with our archenemy. He knows his subtlety; He is aware of his indefatigability and relentlessness. He knows that the devil would curb every move to keep his hold on lost sinners because he owns them: they are his children and he is their father (John 8:44). So, for believers to break through the devil's camp and deliver a sinner, they must have Christ's power or authority. Therefore, Jesus commanded His disciples to tarry in Jerusalem until the promise of the Father came on them. For when the promise of the Father came on them, they would be endued with power to carry out the assignment given to them (Acts 1:8).

Jesus Himself, who was conceived by the Virgin Mary through the Holy Spirit, the only begotten Son of God, fully God and fully man, did not start His earthly ministry until He was baptized with the Holy Spirit. In fact, Christ was ushered into His ministry by the Holy Spirit. We are told in Luke 3:22, *"And the Holy Ghost descended in a bodily shape like a dove upon him, and a voice came from heaven, which said, Thou art my beloved Son; in thee I am well pleased."* Thereby, we are told that Jesus was full of the Holy Spirit (Luke 4:1). All these preceded His earthly ministry. Later in chapter 4 of Luke, as Jesus was teaching in the synagogue, He read from the book of Isaiah (61:1), where it is written of Him concerning His anointing by the Holy Spirit: *"The Spirit of the LORD is upon Me, Because He has anointed Me To preach the gospel to the poor; He has sent Me to heal the brokenhearted, To proclaim liberty to the captives And recovery of sight to the blind, To set at liberty those who are oppressed; To proclaim the acceptable year of the LORD"* (Luke 4:18-19). Also in the book of Acts, we read, *"How God anointed Jesus of Nazareth with the Holy Spirit and with power, who went about doing good and healing all who were oppressed by the devil, for God was with Him"* (Acts 10:3).

If Jesus had to go through this process of waiting for anointing by the Holy Spirit, who are we to carry out His Great Commission without being baptized and filled with the Holy Spirit? Jesus reiterated to the disciples, "Wait until the Holy Spirit comes on you." We too need to wait for the baptism of the Holy Spirit in order to be effective in representing and presenting Him to the dying world.

Speaking in Tongues: Is It for Today?

There have been debates among believers as to whether tongues or speaking in tongues is for today. Some say it has ceased and it was just for the first-century believers. Let's see what the Scriptures say about that.

When the apostles waited or tarried for the baptism with the Holy Spirit as our Lord commanded them, and when the day of Pentecost came, we are told that they were all filled with the Holy Spirit and began to speak with other tongues, as the Spirit gave them utterance (Acts 2:4). When the household of Cornelius were baptized with the Holy Spirit, they also spoke in tongues (Acts 10:46). So did the believers in Ephesus when Paul laid hands on them: they spoke with tongues and prophesied (Acts 19:6).

Now, before Jesus went to be with His Father after commissioning His disciples and also all believers, hear what He said in Mark 16:17: *"And these signs shall follow them that believe; In my name shall they cast out devils; they shall speak with new tongues."* Note what Jesus said here. Who are "them that believe"? They are Christians. Are you a Christian? If yes, then the signs can follow you; however, you must believe. You can speak in new tongues, and you can cast out demons, because the greater One (God) lives in you. It is an experience that is open and available to every believer, but it will not just come if you don't seek or desire it.

People who argue that tongues have ceased tend to base their argument on 1 Corinthians 13:8, which reads, *"Charity never fails: but whether there be prophecies, they shall fail; whether there be tongues, they shall cease; whether there be knowledge, it shall vanish away."* But if we go further to the next verse, it tells us that these things (tongues, prophecies, knowledge, and others) shall vanish *"when that which is perfect is come."* When will that be? It is when Jesus returns. Then we shall no longer "see in a mirror, dimly, but face to face." Hallelujah!

Speaking in tongues is one of the nine gifts of the Spirit described by the Apostle Paul in 1 Corinthians 12, and we will study more about these gifts in the next chapter.

How to Receive the Baptism of the Holy Spirit

1. Repent and believe on Jesus for the remission of your sins: Acts 2:38-39, *"Then Peter said unto them, Repent, and be baptized every one of you in the name of Jesus Christ for the remission of sins, and ye shall receive the gift of the Holy Ghost. For the promise is unto you, and to your children, and to all that are afar off, even as many as the Lord our God shall call."*

2. Ask: Luke 11:13, *"If ye then, being evil, know how to give good gifts unto your children: how much more shall your heavenly Father give the Holy Spirit to them that ask him?"*

3. Believe: Galatians 3:14, *"That the blessing of Abraham might come on the Gentiles through Jesus Christ; that we might receive the promise of the Spirit through faith."* Galatians 3:2, *"This only would I learn of you, Received ye the Spirit by the works of the law, or by the hearing of faith?"*

It should be noted that not everyone will receive the gift in the same way, though it is essential that you repent, ask, and have faith in God's Word as promised. Some people have received the gift by just listening to the Word of God, and some when another Spirit-filled believer lays hands on them. But many have received it by asking.

When you receive the baptism with the Holy Spirit, there is unquestionable assurance that you have received it. It is like finishing a course of study or learning a trade. At the end of the training, you receive a diploma, and there is no question about whether you have received your diploma or not. If anyone asks, "Have you received your diploma?" you either say yes or no! Similarly, if you have received the baptism with the Holy Spirit, you just know it.

Chapter 6

The Gifts of the Spirit

God through the Apostle Paul enlightens us concerning the gifts of the Holy Spirit. Paul says in 1 Corinthians 12:1, *"Concerning spiritual gifts, brethren, I would not have you ignorant."* Unfortunately, many believers today are still in the dark concerning spiritual gifts, and as such the devil robs them of these godly blessings.

> *Now concerning spiritual gifts, brethren, I would not have you ignorant.*
> *Ye know that ye were Gentiles, carried away unto these dumb idols, even as ye were led.*
> *Wherefore I give you to understand, that no man speaking by the Spirit of God calleth Jesus accursed: and that no man can say that Jesus is the Lord, but by the Holy Ghost.*
> *Now there are diversities of gifts, but the same Spirit.*
> *And there are differences of administrations, but the same Lord.*
> *And there are diversities of operations, but it is the same God which worketh all in all.*
> *But the manifestation of the Spirit is given to every man to profit withal.*
> *For to one is given by the Spirit the word of wisdom; to another the word of knowledge by the same Spirit;*
> *To another faith by the same Spirit; to another the gifts of healing by the same Spirit;*
> *To another the working of miracles; to another prophecy; to another discerning of spirits; to another divers kinds of tongues; to another the interpretation of tongues:*
> *But all these worketh that one and the selfsame Spirit, dividing to every man severally as he will.* (1 Corinthians 12:1-11)

What we commonly call spiritual gifts are actually spiritual manifestations. God, who is good and gracious, always reveals His presence among His people. He manifests Himself through these spiritual gifts. That of course gives an important indication that we serve the One and Only living God. Have you ever heard, "thus saith the Lord" in a Muslim or Buddhist meeting, or heard of sick people being brought to them for prayer and healing? Of course, Christianity is not just a religion but a relationship with the Almighty God, the creator of heaven and earth. When Christians have revival meetings, even nonbelievers come for prayer, because God manifests Himself and bears witness that we are in alignment with the work that our Lord Jesus started. In Hebrews 2:4, we read, *"God also bearing them witness, both with signs and wonders, and with divers miracles, and gifts of the Holy Ghost, according to his own will?"*

The spiritual gifts help the body of Christ to function effectively and efficiently. Paul compares the gifts of the Holy Spirit to the human body; all the parts function together for the good of the whole body. For example, if you are hungry and you see a mango tree with ripe fruit, your eyes see it first, you walk there on your feet, and your hand plucks the fruit. But you have yet to enjoy it until your mouth performs its function. Every part has its function; so are the gifts of the Holy Spirit to the body of believers. The manifestations of the Spirit are given to every man to profit from, but the Holy Spirit is absolutely sovereign, and He alone decides how to give these gifts to individual members of the church. All we have to do is to submit or yield to Him. You do not pick a gift and ask Him to qualify you for it. The Bible says we should covet the gifts, but ultimately the Holy Spirit is in charge.

The spiritual gifts enable us to carry out the work Jesus left for us to accomplish on earth. Jesus, who was conceived by the Holy Spirit and anointed with the Holy Spirit while physically here in the world, had to operate under the auspices of the nine gifts of the Holy Spirit. Therefore, we too must do His work under the same umbrella. That is why Jesus said, "Greater works than these shall you do; because I go unto my Father." He meant that by going to His Father, He would send down the Holy Spirit to dwell in us, manifesting Himself through us, enabling us to do great exploits for the kingdom of God.

The gifts are available to the church and every born-again believer, but you must earnestly seek them, as Paul encouraged the Corinthian church. We must desire or be hungry for the gifts. As you know very well, you cannot feed someone who is not hungry. If we don't desire or become hungry for the gifts, the Holy Spirit will not force Himself on anyone. As we seek Him, He will sovereignly distribute the gifts according to His will. He alone has the prerogative to assign these special gifts to the members of the body of Christ.

Some people make the mistake of trying to choose an area and ask the Holy Spirit to use them for certain manifestations. That is not your job. The administration and operation of the gifts are purely His; we are only agents through which the operation is carried out. He divides to every man severally as He wills (1 Corinthians 12:11). They are given for the common good of the church (1 Corinthians 12:7). Only make yourself available, and He will work through you as He wills to the Glory of God. And you are not to become jealous of other members with a gift different from yours. You belong to the same body. The body needs the eyes as well as the ears. They have different functions.

It should be made clear that gifts of the Holy Spirit are not titles, positions, or trophies, but an anointing to carry out the work as the Holy Spirit wills. There are people who use these gifts to promote their interest rather than serve the interest of the Giver.

The Gifts

The nine gifts of the Holy Spirit as given in 1 Corinthians 12 are: the word of wisdom; the word of knowledge; faith; the gifts of healing; the working of miracles; prophecy; discerning of spirits; divers kinds of tongues; and the interpretation of tongues.

The gifts can be further classified into three categories, as shown in the table below:

Category	Gifts	Purpose
Revelation	Word of Wisdom	Reveals God's plan for the future.
	Word of Knowledge	Reveals things in the mind of God (past and present).
	Discerning of Spirits	Supernatural insights into the realms of spirits (both good and evil).
Power	Faith	To passively receive miracles from God.
	Working of Miracles	For believers to perform miracles.
	Gifts of Healing	Divine healing without natural means.

Vocal	Prophecy	Edification, exhortation, and comfort of the church.
	Divers Kinds of Tongues	Edification of the church or individual.
	Interpretation of Tongues	Edification of the church or individual.

The Word of Wisdom

The word of wisdom is a divine revelation by the Holy Spirit concerning God's plan for the future. It is always about the future, unlike the word of knowledge, which speaks of the past or present. Let us carefully look at what verse eight says, "For to one is given by the Spirit the word of wisdom; to another the word of knowledge by the same Spirit." In the first place, it says "word of wisdom" and not "gift of wisdom." It is not natural wisdom, but supernatural. It is not what you acquire through study and then apply. Wisdom in its simplest definition is the application of knowledge. The word of wisdom is a supernatural revelation by the Holy Spirit, and it can be manifested through anyone, young or old, experienced or inexperienced—it is as the Holy Spirit wills.

Secondly, the verse says that to one is given the word of wisdom and to another the word of knowledge; this means not everyone will have the word of wisdom or word of knowledge. All you have to do is to submit to the Holy Spirit, and He will take care of the rest. It is only God who has all wisdom, and He will reveal to us the wisdom we need.

How is the word of wisdom revealed? The word of wisdom can come in many different ways, such as in a vision or dream, or even as an audible voice. It can also come through prophecy, or by tongues and interpretation. In Genesis 6, we have the record of God's plan to deal with the wickedness of man on earth. God revealed His plan to Noah and told him exactly what to do in order to escape the destruction that was ahead. The revelation here was the word of wisdom, and it came to him through an audible voice. God will not leave man without providing a way of escape. Destruction comes when we refuse to heed His warnings. Rejecting God's instructions and warnings has always been the problem of man.

We also see in the Pentateuch that God spoke to Moses several times. For example, God gave Moses the law in an audible voice, and it gave God's plan and purpose for Israel, which is, of course, the word of wisdom.

God gave Joseph a supernatural revelation through a dream of what was coming in the future and what to do. Later Joseph would say to his brethren, "God sent me before you to preserve posterity for you in the earth, and to save your lives by a great deliverance." The dream was obviously a word of wisdom. Daniel also received the word of wisdom through a dream.

The prophets in the Old Testament received the word of wisdom through prophecy. Many of them prophesied concerning God's future plan for the salvation of mankind through the coming Messiah, Jesus Christ. Isaiah wrote, *"Therefore the Lord himself shall give you a sign; Behold, a virgin shall conceive, and bear a son, and shall call his name Immanuel"* (Isaiah 7:14).

The Word of Wisdom in the New Testament:

The Holy Spirit uses two additional mediums to manifest Himself in the New Testament that are not found in the Old Testament. These are tongues and the interpretation of tongues. Speaking in tongues was promised by Jesus Christ, and it came to believers on the day of Pentecost. Tongues and the interpretation of tongues are prophetic utterances; both oral prophesying and speaking in tongues occur when the Holy Spirit comes upon someone and prompts the person to speak. The basic difference is that prophesying is in the speaker's own language, whereas speaking in tongues is in a language unknown to the speaker. We shall discuss this more under the vocal gifts.

We have several manifestations of the word of wisdom in the New Testament. An example is the vision that John the Apostle had on the Isle of Patmos, when the Lord revealed to him the condition of the seven churches in Asia Minor. The first part of the vision showed the present condition of the churches; this is the word of knowledge, which we shall discuss shortly. But where the word of wisdom comes in is the instructions given to the church about how to fulfill God's plan and purpose for them.

Another manifestation of the word of wisdom was to Philip (Acts 8:26-39), one of the deacons chosen along with Stephen. In his revelation, it was an angel of God that came to him to deliver the message. God had a plan to expand His word in Ethiopia, so he instructed Philip to go down from Jerusalem unto Gaza, and there he was able to meet the Ethiopian eunuch, thereby fulfilling God's plan.

Natural Wisdom versus Word of Wisdom:

The word of wisdom must be differentiated from natural wisdom, which has to do with the affairs of life. As we have seen in 1 Corinthians 12:8, the word of wisdom and any other gifts of the Holy Spirit are supernatural manifestations and are given as He wills. Not everyone will have the gift of the word of wisdom or word of knowledge. But everyone can have natural wisdom, and if you lack wisdom, the Bible tells us how to receive it. James 1:5 (NKJV) says, *"If any of you lacks wisdom, let him ask of God, who gives to all liberally and without reproach, and it will be given to him."* This is the wisdom we need for dealing prudently with the things in life.

The key to getting wisdom so as to be successful in the things of life is what God told Joshua: *"This Book of the Law shall not depart out of your mouth, but you shall meditate on it day and night, that you may observe and do according to all that is written in it. For then you shall make your way prosperous, and then you shall deal wisely and have good success"* (Joshua 1:8, Amplified). King Solomon admonishes us to heed instruction and be wise, and not to neglect it (Proverbs 8:33).

What are we to do when the word of wisdom is given? When God gives the word of wisdom, especially when it has to do with consequences of sin, He provides a way to avert the repercussions. The Word of God says, "The soul who sins shall die." He provided a means of escape through His Son Jesus, but you have to repent and believe in His provision for salvation, not in anyone else's. When the children of Israel were bitten by poisonous snakes in the wilderness because of sin, many died. When they cried unto God, He made provision for the consequences of their sin by asking anyone bitten to look on the raised brazen serpent and be healed. Those who refused to simply look at the brazen serpent died.

The Word of Knowledge

The word of knowledge is the divine revelation by the Holy Spirit of certain facts in the mind of God. It is not an intellectual knowledge: it is knowledge revealed by the Holy Spirit to a spirit-filled believer. It is not natural knowledge, but supernatural. This gift is called the word of knowledge and not the gift of knowledge. God is the only One who is omniscient, all-knowing, and the Holy Spirit reveals just a fragment of what we need to know about a subject. Therefore, no human being can boast of having all knowledge about a thing. It is only God who made all things and knows all things.

How Does the Holy Spirit Manifest Himself through the Word of Knowledge?

The word of knowledge can be manifested in a number of different ways, similar to the word of wisdom. It can come through dreams, visions, tongues and interpretation, prophecy, or an angel coming to deliver it. God has infinite ways of doing things, so we cannot limit Him. Often the gifts operate together just like our body: the parts function together for the common good of the whole body.

The manifestation of the word of knowledge through a vision can be seen in Acts 10, where we are told that Peter went up on the roof to pray and fell into a trance and saw heaven opened. While he was pondering within himself what the vision meant, the Holy Spirit spoke to him, saying that three men were seeking him and that he should rise and go with them. There was no way Peter could have known these men were seeking him without the manifestation of the word of knowledge through his vision.

Jesus Himself operated with all the gifts of the Holy Spirit. He is the only One to whom God gave the Spirit without measure (John 3:34). When Jesus was at the well in Samaria, it was through the word of knowledge that He convinced the Samaritan woman of her sin. Jesus told her to go and call her husband and come back, and she answered, "I have no husband." Through the word of knowledge, which came by inward revelation, Jesus told her that she had had five husbands and the one she was living with was not her husband. The woman quickly said, "Sir, I perceive that You are a prophet." Jesus had inward revelation through the gift of the word of knowledge.

We must be very careful not to confuse the word of knowledge with a profound knowledge of the Bible, which comes through the study of the Word and a close walk with God. When we have a close relationship with God, in His kindness He reveals some of His ways to us. In Psalm 103:7, we are told that He made known his ways unto Moses, his acts unto the children of Israel. Also, in Psalm 25:14, we read, *"The secret of the Lord is with them that fear him; and he will shew them his covenant."* However, the word of knowledge is a supernatural revelation and does not necessarily come from a long walk or experience with God. An example can be seen in 1 Samuel 3. Here, the boy Samuel was ministering unto the Lord under the priest Eli. The Lord called Samuel, and he ran to Eli and said, "Here I am." He was yet a child and had no experience of such a call from God. After he was called and ran to Eli three times, Eli perceived that the Lord was calling him, so he told Samuel whenever he heard a call again, he should say, "Speak, for your servant is listening." Eli knew that God must be calling Samuel. This was natural knowledge that he acquired by experience.

The Discerning of Spirits

The gift of discerning of spirits is the third gift in the revelation group. It gives supernatural insights into the realm of spirits. In the spirit world, there are good spirits and evil spirits. The two gifts we considered earlier, the word of wisdom and word of knowledge, are much broader in scope and application than discerning of spirits. Since the word of wisdom gives us a revelation of the mind and purpose of God, I rank it first, followed by the word of knowledge, which gives us a revelation of things in the present or past.

We must be diligent in calling this gift what the Bible calls it. It is not discerning of demons or evil spirits, and the Bible has not called it the gift of discernment. There are some things we know through the Spirit of God and erroneously call the gift of discernment when it is actually the word of knowledge in operation. This gift is also not mind reading or psychological insight— there are some who are quick at discerning faults in people and call that a gift of discerning spirits. This is not what Paul is talking about; that is against the Word of God (Matthew 7:1). The Bible calls it the gift of discerning of spirits, both good and evil spirits.

This gift can manifest in the same ways as the word of wisdom and word of knowledge. Many believers have supernaturally seen the risen Christ through visions and dreams, but we know Christ is seated at the right hand of the Father (Hebrews 12:2)—this is the discerning of spirits.

When the prophet Isaiah saw the Lord sitting upon a throne with His angelic beings, this was discerning of spirits in operation. *"In the year that king Uzziah died I saw also the Lord sitting upon a throne, high and lifted up, and his train filled the temple. Above it stood the seraphims: each one had six wings; with twain he covered his face, and with twain he covered his feet, and with twain he did fly. And one cried unto another, and said, Holy, holy, holy, is the LORD of hosts: the whole earth is full of his glory"* (Isaiah 6:1-3).

The vision that John saw on the Isle of Patmos concerning the seven Spirits before the throne of God in chapters three and four was a manifestation of the discerning of spirits. He was seeing into the spirit realm and saw seven facets of the Spirit of God.

Paul was able to discern the kind of spirit in a slave girl in Philippi who was possessed with a spirit of divination. For many days she kept following Paul and the rest, shouting, *"These men are servants of the Most High God, who are telling you the way to be saved"* (Acts 16:16-18). At first appearance, you would have thought the spirit was of the Lord. But Paul with the gift of discerning of spirits knew it was an unclean spirit, and he rebuked the spirit and commanded it to come out of her, and at that moment the spirit left her.

Well, you may say, how will I know if a spirit is of God or Satan if I do not have the gift of discerning of spirits? In the first place, at your rebirth into the family of God, you receive the indwelling of the Holy Spirit, and He guides you through your spirit. Proverbs 20:27 says, *"The spirit of man is the candle of the Lord, searching all the inward parts of the belly"* Also in Romans 8:16, *"The Spirit itself bears witness with our spirit, that we are the children of God."* Therefore, we have inward witness that reveals the truth to us, whether it be of God or Satan.

We now come to the second group of gifts of the Holy Spirit, the power group, comprising the gift of faith, the working of miracles, and the gifts of healing. The greatest of these three gifts is the gift of faith, because it is the mechanism for the other two.

The Gift of Faith

The gift of faith is a supernatural conviction of God's power and promises, unshaken by circumstances and obstacles that enables us to accomplish His will and purpose with confidence in Him and His Word. People with this gift see their words honored by God just as His, and miraculously bring them to actuality.

Before delving into the gift of faith, or special faith, as some refer to it, we need to understand that there are several levels or kinds of faith mentioned in Scripture. The Bible talks about strong faith, common faith, weak faith, little faith, growing faith, genuine faith, wavering faith, unwavering faith, great faith, and others.

Hebrews 11:1 defines faith as *"the confidence in what we hope for and assurance about what we do not see."* Abraham, who is known as the father of faith, exercised strong faith in God, who promised him even in his old age that he would have a child through his wife, who had been barren and was well advanced in age. They did not get the promised child until it was biologically impossible. But the kind of faith Abraham had does not entertain impossibility.

Saving Faith:

The saving faith is what God gives to everyone that comes to Him, and that is what leads us to salvation. We are told in Ephesians 2:8-9: *"For by grace are ye saved through faith; and that not of yourselves: it is the gift of God: Not of works, lest any man should boast."* And how does this faith come? It comes by hearing and hearing by the Word of God (Romans 10:17).

Common Faith:

Common faith or general faith is shared by all believers. Paul tells us that God has dealt to each one a measure of faith (Romans 12:3). This common faith can be increased by feeding on the Word of God and exercising it in every facet of our life: *"As newborn babes, desire the sincere milk of the word, that ye may grow thereby"* (1 Peter 2:2).

Additionally, common faith is the faith we need to receive answers to our prayers. If answers to all prayers required the gift of faith, then most people would not receive anything from God, because the Bible says "to another faith by the same Spirit." That means not everyone will have the gift of faith. But always remember that God gives these gifts for the benefit of the church.

Genuine Faith:

Genuine faith is a sincere faith from a honest heart to do what is right no matter the situation or condition. We have an example of Timothy's grandmother Lois and his mother Eunice.

"When I call to remembrance the genuine faith that is in you, which dwelt first in your grandmother Lois and your mother Eunice and I am persuaded is in you also" (2 Timothy 1:5).

Strong Faith:

The Bible said of Abraham that he was strong in faith, and giving glory to God while he still awaited the promise, he was persuaded that the promised cannot fail and there is no impossibility with Him. He did not stagger or become weak in faith. He believed that once God said it, it was settled. The Psalmist said, *"Forever, O LORD, thy word is settled in heaven"* (Psalm 119:89).

This is the promise of God that Abraham believed: *"(As it is written, I have made thee a father of many nations,) before him whom he believed, even God, who quickeneth the dead, and calleth those things which be not as though they were. Who against hope believed in hope, that he might become the father of many nations, according to that which was spoken, So shall thy seed be. And being not weak in faith, he considered not his own body now dead, when he was about an hundred years old, neither yet the deadness of Sara's womb: He staggered not at the promise of God through unbelief; but was strong in faith, giving glory to God; And being fully persuaded that, what he had promised, he was able also to perform"* (Romans 4:1-21).

Little Faith:

This kind of faith lacks complete or total trust in God. It is always anxious and tends to be fearful. Jesus said in Matthew 8:26, *"Why are you fearful, O you of little faith? Then He arose and rebuked the winds and the sea, and there was a great calm."* Paul admonishes us in Philippians 4:6, *"Be anxious for nothing, but in everything by prayer and supplication, with thanksgiving, let your requests be made known to God."*

Great Faith:

Jesus used the term "great faith" for two non-Jews, a centurion whose servant was sick and a Canaanite woman whose daughter was demon-possessed. This is an indefatigable and totally convinced kind of faith. It does not give up until the prayer is answered.

"The centurion answered and said, Lord, I am not worthy that thou shouldest come under my roof: but speak the word only, and my servant shall be healed. For I am a man under authority, having soldiers under me: and I say to this man, Go, and he goeth; and to another, Come, and he cometh; and to my servant, Do this, and he doeth it. When Jesus heard it, he marveled, and said to them that followed, Verily I say unto you, I have not found so great faith, no, not in Israel." (Matthew 8:8-10).

The Canaanite woman whose daughter was demon-possessed came to Jesus begging for mercy for her daughter to be set free, and Jesus told her that He was sent only to the lost sheep of Israel. The woman did not say "Okay, I cannot do anything," and turn back, but persisted and replied with faith-filled words: "But even the dogs eat the crumbs that fall from their masters' table." Seeing her unrelenting faith, Jesus answered, *"O woman, great is thy faith: be it unto thee even as thou wilt. And her daughter was made whole from that very hour"* (Matthew 15:28).

The Gift of Faith:

The gift of faith is not for everyone (1 Corinthians 12:9). The Holy Spirit gives as He wills, and this gift is a supernatural manifestation of the Holy Spirit for the benefit of the body of Christ and must exalt the head, Jesus Christ. By this gift a believer passively receives a miracle. This gift of faith is separate and distinct from saving faith, common faith, or any other kind of faith. For example, common faith can be increased by feeding on the Word of God and exercising it, but the gift of faith is a supernatural manifestation, and those who operate in it believe God in a way that He honors their words as His word. There are several instances in both the Old and New Testaments when the gift of faith was manifested. As we will see, the gift of faith can operate in many ways, such as divine protection, provision, raising the dead, or casting out demons.

In the book of Daniel, we see the miraculous deliverance of three Hebrew men, Shadrach, Meshach, and Abednego. These men refused to bow down and worship King Nebuchadnezzar's idol, and they were bound and thrown into the midst of a burning fiery furnace. But they were miraculously loosed inside the fire and began to walk freely without being burnt, and not a hair of their heads was singed, nor were their coats changed, nor did they have the smell of fire on them. This was a great miracle they received from God because they trusted in the living God. Nebuchadnezzar, a godless king, testified later and said, *"Blessed be the God of Shadrach, Meshach, and Abednego, who hath sent his angel, and delivered his servants that trusted in him, and have changed the king's word, and yielded their bodies, that they might not serve nor worship any god, except their own God"* (Daniel 3:28).

Daniel himself received a miraculous deliverance when he was thrown into the lions' den (Daniel 6). This is, of course, the gift of faith in operation, where he passively received deliverance from God; he did not do anything but simply trust his God. We read in verse 23 that "no manner of hurt was found upon him, because he believed in his God." Daniel said God sent His angel and shut the lions' mouths. Why? Because of Daniel's faith in God. He must have calmly and sweetly slept with the lions. There is no record that anyone else ever thrown into the lions' den came back alive. In fact, when those who had falsely accused Daniel were thrown into the lions' den with their families, we are told that the lions overpowered them and crushed all their bones. Those who operate with this special faith have always exhibited calm in their situation, no matter the outcome.

The miraculous sustenance of Elijah during the famine is another gift of faith in operation. It is unheard of that a bird could in a timely manner bring breakfast and dinner to a man. It is not natural, but a divine arrangement. *"The ravens brought him bread and flesh in the morning, and bread and flesh in the evening; and he drank of the brook"* (1 Kings 17:6).

In the New Testament, we read about Jesus operating within the gift of faith when He went to sleep in the back of a ship during a great tempest (Matthew 8:23–27).

Did Jesus need to operate within the gift of faith even though He is the Son of God? Yes. All the wonderful things Jesus did while He walked on earth were done through the power of the Holy Spirit. If He were not operating as a man, He wouldn't be sleeping, because God does not get tired or sleep. Jesus never did anything but by the power of the Holy

Spirit. He stripped Himself of power as the Son of God and ministered as a man anointed by the Spirit. Jesus was not bothered by the storm, just as Daniel was not bothered by the lions. They both lay down and slept right there in the face of danger.

The Apostle Peter had the same kind of calm when he was imprisoned; he knew he could be killed the following day, yet slept soundly until an angel of the Lord woke him up and led him out of the prison (Acts 12). Many Christians have been martyred for the sake of the gospel in many places throughout the world, and there are those who have been burned at the stake. Even the night before, many were so calm that they lay down and slept all night before being taken to the stake. That's the gift of faith in operation.

In the Apostolic era and even today, unclean spirits have been cast out, and this is an example of the gift of faith in operation. When Paul cast out the unclean spirit from the slave girl who earned money for her owners by fortune-telling, the gift of faith was involved. In this instance, you are trusting God to honor your word when you command an unclean spirit to come out in the name of Jesus. Of course, when you cast out demonic spirits, other gifts of the Spirit are in operation too, such as the discerning of spirits or word of knowledge. In any case, the gift of faith still has to be exercised while casting out the evil spirits.

The operation of the gift of faith has been documented by many writers in the ministry of Smith Wigglesworth, who was said to have raised several people who have literally died. One of them was his wife. It was reported that one day when he arrived home from work, he was met at the door with news that his wife had been dead for two hours. To that Wigglesworth replied, "No, she's not dead." He dropped his lunch bucket and tools, walked into the bedroom, pulled her out of bed, stood her against the wall, called her by her first name, and said, "I command you to come to me now!" Then he backed off, and here she came! She lived a number of years after that.

The Working of Miracles

"To another the working of miracles" (1 Corinthians 12:10).

As mentioned previously, the gift of faith allows a believer to receive miracles, but the gift of working miracles allows a believer to perform or work miracles. One gift receives, and the other gift does something. These gifts are closely associated, just like the gifts of revelation and the vocal or utterance gifts.

The working of miracles is a supernatural power to intervene in the ordinary course of nature and the common natural law that governs the material world. It is faith that triggers a miracle. For example, Elisha made an iron axe-head float on water; this is a miracle because by natural law, iron should not float on water. Its density is higher than that of water.

We must first of all understand the word "miracle" as used in the phrase "working of miracles." Since we encounter the word almost every day in advertisements for products such as "Miracle Whip," "miracle detergent," and so on, if we are not careful, we might lose the meaning as used here. The Greek word translated as "miracle" is *dunamis*. From this same Greek word comes the English word "dynamite," which is a chemical explosive that has the inherent power to level a whole building within a second. The working of miracles means doing things that are otherwise impossible or contrary to the laws of nature.

In the Old Testament we see more of the working of miracles, while in the New Testament we see more of the gifts of healing. One of the reasons we see more manifestations of healing in the New Testament is the declaration of Jesus in Mark 16:18 that believers shall lay hands on the sick and they shall recover. In the Old Testament, it was mainly the leaders and prophets whom God used in the working of miracles.

We begin to see the working of miracles by God through Moses and his brother Aaron, who delivered the children of Israel from bondage in Egypt. There were ten miracles known as the ten plagues that occurred before Pharaoh could let God's people go. Along the journey, the Red Sea divided (Exodus 14:16), and Moses also brought water out of the rock (Exodus 17:1-6). Joshua, who became the leader after Moses' death, did some working of miracles, such as crossing the Jordan River on dry land (Joshua 3:15-17) and making the sun stand still (Joshua 10:12-13). The prophet Elijah did several miracles too, such as making a handful of meal and a little oil miraculously feed the widow woman of Zarephath with her household during a drought that lasted three years. He restored a child who had died to life through prayer (1 Kings 17), and he prayed down fire from heaven (1 Kings 18:37-38). Elisha, who received the double portion of his master Elijah, performed several miracles: multiplying oil for a poor woman (2 Kings 4), healing a bitter spring in Jericho (2 Kings 2), raising a child from the dead (2 Kings 4), cleansing Naaman the Syrian of his leprosy (2 Kings 5), and making the axe-head float on water (2 Kings 6).

In the New Testament, we see many miracles throughout the ministry of Jesus. The first miracle recorded is in John 2:1-11 at the wedding in Cana, where He turned water to wine. Jesus calmed the stormy sea in Matthew 8:23-26. Jesus walked on water and made Peter walk on water too (Matthew 14:22-

31). Jesus fed many people with a boy's lunch (John 6:5-14). Jesus raised Lazarus from the dead (John 11:1-44).

The apostles continued where Jesus left off, and several miracles were seen in their ministry. Peter and John, for example, made the lame walk (Acts 3). We read in Acts 6:8 that Stephen, full of faith and power, did great wonders and miracles among the people. And in Acts 8:6, Philip, also a deacon, performed miracles. In Acts 19, God did extraordinary miracles through Paul in the province of Asia, to the extent that when handkerchiefs and aprons that had touched him were taken to the sick, their illnesses were cured and the evil spirits left those that were possessed.

Purpose for the Working of Miracles:

People are always attracted to miracles because they enjoy the unusual, and some want them for selfish reasons. However, the working of miracles, like any other spiritual gift, is meant to bring glory to the name of God and for the good of His body—the church. Jesus did not just perform or work miracles for the sake of doing it. On one occasion certain Pharisees and scribes came to Jesus and said, "Master, we want to see a miraculous sign from you." He answered, *"An evil and adulterous generation seeketh after a sign; and there shall no sign be given to it, but the sign of the prophet Jonas"* (Matthew 12:39). During the trial of Jesus, we read that Herod was exceedingly glad to see Jesus, hoping he would see Jesus perform some miracle. Jesus equally rebuked James and John when they wanted him to perform a miracle by calling fire down from heaven to consume those who rejected Him.

The working of miracles must bring honor to God and fulfill His will and purpose. When the Israelites were going to the land God promised them, they came to the Red Sea, and behind them was Pharaoh's army, and they had nowhere to turn. They needed miraculous intervention from God. God will always honor His word, so He performed a miracle through Moses, causing the sea to part for the Israelites to cross safely. When the Egyptians tried to cross like the people of God, they were drowned.

Similarly, God uses miracles to remove barriers to the gospel. We see some examples in the book of Acts. In Acts 5, the prison doors miraculously opened for the apostles who were locked up for preaching the gospel; God did not want to see the hindrance of the gospel message, so He had to perform this miracle. In Acts 13, when Paul and Barnabas were preaching the gospel to the proconsul Sergius Paulus, Elymas the sorcerer tried to turn him from the faith, and God had to perform a miracle through Paul to bring blindness on Elymas so as to remove the hindrance.

The Gifts of Healing

The gifts of healing are supernatural manifestations of the healing power of God without natural means or the use of any medicine.

"To another faith by the same Spirit; to another the gifts of healing by the same Spirit; And God hath set some in the church, first apostles, secondarily prophets, thirdly teachers, after that miracles, then gifts of healings, helps, governments, diversities of tongues. Are all apostles? Are all prophets? Are all teachers? Are all workers of miracles? Have all the gifts of healing? Do all speak with tongues? Do all interpret?" (1 Corinthians 12:9, 28-30).

As seen in the Scriptural verses above, the gifts of healing are not for everyone. As with the other spiritual gifts, the Holy Spirit is the Giver and He distributes as He wills for the glory of God and for the benefit of the body of Christ. You will also notice that it is written in plural form as "gifts of healing" in all three verses, not as "gift of healing." Many great Bible teachers like Rev. Kenneth E. Hagin and Howard Carter have discussed the lack of a reason for the distinction between this gift and the other gifts. Howard Carter says, "It may well be that gifts mean that certain believers are used by the Holy Spirit to heal certain kinds of sickness, disease or infirmity."

Though the gifts of healing are not for everyone, it does not mean you cannot pray for others or yourself and receive divine healing. You do not have to receive the gifts of healing before God heals you. All you need is faith in God (Mark 11:20-24). And that is why James wrote: *"Is any sick among you? Let him call for the elders of the church; and let them pray over him, anointing him with oil in the name of the Lord: And the prayer of faith shall save the sick, and the Lord shall raise him up; and if he have committed sins, they shall be forgiven him. Confess your faults one to another, and pray one for another, that ye may be healed"* (James 5:14-16).

Purpose for Healing:

Throughout the ministry of Jesus, the gifts of healing and working of miracles were always in operation and attracted many people to come and hear the good news. The crowds saw miraculous supplies of food many times, where thousands were fed with just a child's lunch. They also saw many people healed. In Luke 4:40, we are told that all those who were sick with various diseases were brought to Jesus, and He laid His hands on every one of them and healed them. Even today, any evangelistic ministry that operates with the gifts of healing will attract people to come and hear the Word of God and receive divine healing. So, we see the gifts of healing serving two purposes: (1) setting people free from sickness and disease, and (2) bringing the Word of God to them for their salvation.

God Is Always Willing to Heal:

Divine healing comes from God but flows through a believer to individuals who need it. Howard Carter said it is better to say that "by the Holy Spirit and through the Spirit-filled believer, gifts of healing are manifested in the church." It is always the will of God to heal, just as much as He is always willing to forgive us our sins. Psalm 103:3 says, *"Who forgiveth all thine iniquities; who healeth all thy diseases."* The man who was covered with leprosy came to Jesus and said, *"'Lord, if you are willing, you can make me clean.' Jesus reached out His hand and touched the man and said, 'I am willing'"* (Luke 5:13, NIV). Jesus took our infirmities and bore our sicknesses (Matthew 8:17). Jesus was so concerned about healing the sick that He gave power to His disciples to cast out unclean spirits and to heal all manner of sickness and disease (Matthew 10:1). Healing includes casting out demons, curing, and renewing the whole body and mind.

Faith is always needed to trigger the healing or working of miracles, so you can see that the power gifts are closely associated. On one occasion, the faith of the person being healed was a factor (Matthew 9:22). At other times, the faith of a friend or family member contributed (Matthew 15:28; Mark 2:5, 11). The faith of the person who prays for the healing plays an important role in becoming healed (Mark 9:17-24, James 5:15). The important thing to remember is that God wants us healed.

Now we come to the gifts of inspiration or vocal spiritual gifts, which comprise prophecy, different kinds of tongues, and the interpretation of tongues. Of these three gifts, prophecy ranks highest because the other two equate to prophecy. Paul himself said, *"He that prophesies is greater than he that speaks in tongues, unless he interprets"* (1 Corinthians 14:5).

Prophecy

Prophecy can be defined as a supernatural utterance in a known tongue. Its primary purpose in the church today is for edification, exhortation, and comfort (1 Corinthians 14:3).

In the Old Testament, there were only a few instances when those who prophesied were not prophets. The first instance was when Moses told God that he needed help with the children of Israel he was leading to the promised land. God asked him to gather seventy elders, and He took the Spirit on Moses and put it on them, and they began to prophesy (Numbers 11:25-29). The second time was with Saul, the king of Israel. *"And it came to pass, when all that knew him beforetime saw that, behold, he prophesied among the prophets, then the people said one to another, What is this that is come unto the son of Kish? Is Saul also among the prophets?"* (1 Samuel 10:11). These people prophesied because the Holy Spirit of God came upon them.

The Hebrew word for prophet (*nabiy*) means a spokesman or a speaker who solemnly declares to the people what he has received by inspiration. Therefore, a prophet is someone who speaks for God—His mouthpiece. The word is first used in the Bible in Genesis 20:7 by God Himself concerning Abraham, when God appeared to Abimelech king of Gerar in a dream concerning Sarah. God said, *"For he is a prophet, and he shall pray for you."*

God said to Moses that his brother Aaron should be a prophet unto him (Exodus 7:1). Miriam, the sister of Aaron, was also a prophetess (Exodus 15:20). The Bible narrative tells us about prophets like Samuel, Nathan, Elijah, Elisha, and others. The canon also contains written prophecy ascribed to prophets like Isaiah, Jeremiah, Ezekiel, Daniel, and others. The prophets moved the story forward from Moses through the conquest of Canaan into the era of kings, and then into the exile and eventual return to the promised land.

In the New Testament, every believer who is baptized in the Holy Spirit can prophesy if they desire or covet it (1 Corinthians 14:39). It should be noted that not everyone who prophesies is a prophet. To be called a prophet, you have to be called by God to that office and receive additional spiritual gifts such as the word of wisdom, word of knowledge, or discerning of spirits. Paul says, *"God has appointed these in the church: first apostles, second prophets, and third teachers"* (1 Corinthians 12:28).

Is prophecy still for us today? The answer is yes! Some people think that because there are false prophets, we should not pay attention to prophecy today. Even in the Old Testament, there were false prophets. Hear the warning of God concerning false prophets: *"But the prophet, which shall presume to speak a word in my name, which I have not commanded him to speak, or that shall speak in the name of other gods, even that prophet shall die"* (Deuteronomy 18:20). The fact that we have fake money does not stop us from spending money. And the fact that we have false prophets proves there are genuine ones.

In the book of Joel God said, *"And it shall come to pass afterward, that I will pour out my spirit upon all flesh; and your sons and your daughters shall prophesy, your old men shall dream dreams, your young men shall see visions"* (Joel 2:28).

Divers Kinds of Tongues

Speaking in different kinds of tongues and interpretation of tongues are gifts of the Holy Spirit that never occurred in the Old Testament. Speaking in tongues first occurred on the day of Pentecost as a sign of baptism in the Holy Spirit. However, the promise was made by our Lord in Mark 16:17 that believers shall speak with new tongues.

The gift of different kinds of tongues is a supernatural utterance in unknown languages. The languages are never learned by the speaker, and not perceived in his mind or intellect. It is purely a miraculous utterance that occurs when the Holy Spirit comes upon someone and prompts him to speak.

This gift that Paul is talking about here is not for everyone: *"to another divers kinds of tongues"* (1 Corinthians 12:10). However, the ability to speak in tongues is for everyone who believes in Jesus Christ, as He promised in Mark 16:17. Why do we need the tongues? Romans 8:26 tells us that *"the Spirit also helps in our weaknesses for we do not know what we should pray for as we ought, but the Spirit Himself makes intercession for us with groanings which cannot be uttered."* Jude also admonishes us to pray in the Holy Spirit (Jude 1:20). When we speak in tongues we are not talking to men, but to God.

In 1 Corinthians 14:2, Paul said, *"For he that speaketh in an unknown tongue speaketh not unto men, but unto God: for no man understandeth him; howbeit in the spirit he speaketh mysteries."*

For group edification, Paul emphasized that there must be interpretation of tongues. In 1 Corinthians 14:5, he said, *"I would that ye all spake with tongues, but rather that ye prophesied: for greater is he that prophesieth than he that speaketh with tongues, except he interpret, that the church may receive edifying."* And in verse twenty-eight, he said if there is no one to interpret, the speaker should keep quiet in the church and speak to himself and God. However, he warns us not to forbid speaking in tongues (1 Corinthians 14:39) and not to quench the Spirit (1 Thessalonians 5:19).

God is sovereign and he knows how to reach out to an individual or group. I heard of an instance where there was a manifestation of tongues in a group, and the language spoken happened to be that of someone in the meeting. This man was highly edified, and encouraged. Immediately after the meeting, he went to the speaker and started speaking his language, not knowing he could not speak a word or understand a word in his language. He said to him, "You spoke so eloquently in my language." This was what happened on the day of Pentecost: *"Now when this was noised abroad, the multitude came together, and were confounded, because that every man heard them speak in his own language. And they were all amazed and marvelled, saying one to another, Behold, are not all these which speak Galilaeans? And how hear we every man in our own tongue, wherein we were born?"* (Acts 2:6-8)

Interpretation of Tongues

This is a supernatural revelation of the meaning of an utterance spoken in an unknown tongue. It is not translation, but interpretation; that is why sometimes the interpreter might be lengthy or vice versa. It is as the Holy Spirit reveals. Translation will be about converting word for word. At times, the interpreter might even go into prophecy after giving the meaning of the tongues if the Holy Spirit inspires him. This is purely the work of the Holy Spirit. I have been blessed to interpret tongues as the Spirit gives me utterance. Do I interpret every tongue? No! It is purely the work of the Holy Spirit and He uses whoever He wants.

Furthermore, Paul encourages those who speak in tongues to pray that they may interpret. This is not just for groups, but in your own private prayer; many times the Spirit has explained to me what I said in tongues. But interpretation is more important in a group setting. See what Paul said in 1 Corinthians 14:23-24: *"So if the whole church comes together and everyone speaks in tongues, and some who do not understand or some unbelievers come in, will they not say that you are out of your mind? But if an unbeliever or someone who does not understand comes in while everybody is prophesying, he will be convinced by all that he is a sinner and will be judged by all."*

Also, Paul in Ephesians 6:18 encourages us to pray always with all prayer and supplication in the Spirit. And Jude 1:20 says, *"But you, beloved, building yourselves up on your most holy faith, praying in the Holy Spirit."* What helps us do that is praying in tongues.

Chapter 7

The Fruit of the Spirit

"But the fruit of the Spirit is love, joy, peace, patience, kindness, goodness, faithfulness, gentleness and self-control. Against such things there is no law" (Galatians 5:22-23, NIV).

In the previous chapter we studied the nine gifts of the Holy Spirit. In this chapter we shall deal with the nine characteristics of the fruit of the Spirit. You will note that Galatians 5:22-23 says "the fruit of the Spirit" and not "the fruit of believers," meaning the fruit is not produced by Christians, but by the Holy Spirit. No Christian can produce the fruit. All efforts or good works to produce the fruit simply lead to futility.

It is fair to say that the life of Christ lived out by a believer brings forth the fruit of the Spirit. In John 15:4-5, we read: *"Abide in me, and I in you. As the branch cannot bear fruit of itself, except it abide in the vine; no more can ye, except ye abide in me. I am the vine, ye are the branches: He that abideth in me, and I in him, the same bringeth forth much fruit: for without me ye can do nothing."*

Secondly, the "fruit" is in singular form—it is not "fruits"—telling us that the nine characteristics of the fruit represent a unity, and all are to be seen in a believer's life. When the world tastes this fruit, they can feel all the characteristics of Christ. Everything is well mixed and balanced. When you taste a good fruit or soup, you just know it. The Psalmist says, *"Taste and see that the Lord is good"* (Psalm 34:8).

As I was meditating on the difference between the gifts and fruit of the Holy Spirit, the first question that came to my mind was "Which of the two is greater or more important?"

Immediately, the story of the fig tree in Mark 11 came to my mind. Jesus cursed this tree, and as He and His disciples passed by the tree the following day, Peter noticed that the fig tree had withered. Why was the tree cursed? Jesus expected to get fruit from the tree for food, but it was fruitless. The tree of course had beautiful leaves, which represent a gift, because not all trees have good leaves to provide shade for people or animals. But when you are hungry and in need of food, you want the fruit. The leaves will not do you any good when you are starving for food.

Believers with gifts but without the fruit of the Spirit will not do much good for a world that is hungry for spiritual food. People need true love instead of hatred in this sometimes miserable world filled with sin, dominated by the heartless dictator, the god of this world—Satan. But his end is at hand. Jesus will come back, as He said, to set up His everlasting kingdom. Before then, let the image of Christ be formed in us so that we can say like Paul: *"For to me to live is Christ, and to die is gain"* (Philippians 1:21).

The nine virtues of the fruit of the Spirit can be classified into three groups, like the gifts of the Holy Spirit.

Virtues	Actions
Love, Joy, and Peace	Habits of Mind (Behavior of Mind)
Patience, Kindness, and Goodness	Reach to Others
Faithfulness, Gentleness, and Temperance	General Conduct

Love

Love is at the top of the list because it is the foundation for all other virtues. All other virtues can actually be found in love.

The term "love" is usually used to express an emotional attraction between two or more people. The word "love" appears in the Bible more than three hundred times, but can be classified into three types: brotherly love (philos), erotic love (eros), and divine love (agape).

Philos:

This is brotherly love: the type of love usually found between blood brothers or sisters and between very close friends. It is also the type of love that you see among many Christians. As great as this kind of love may be, it sometimes ends up being bitter; therefore, it is not always reliable. It is not the God-kind of love.

Eros:

This is the sexual love that comes as a strong feeling between male and female. In Greek mythology, Eros is the name of the god of love (erotic love). God created the desire for sexual love between husband and wife (man and woman), which is important for a healthy relationship. However, as we see it nowadays, couples easily fall out of love because sexual love is mostly self-benefiting, and once it is lost some couples separate.

Agape:

This is the God-kind of love. It is the type of love that God has towards His Son, and mankind. This is the love that made God give His only begotten Son to the world to die for our sins (John 3:16). This is the love expected from all believers who abide in Christ (John 15).

Paul describes this God-kind of love (agape) in 1 Corinthians 13:4-8, NIV:

> *Love is patient,*
> *Love is kind.*
> *Love does not envy,*
> *Love does not boast,*
> *Love is not proud.*
> *Love is not rude,*
> *Love is not self-seeking,*
> *Love is not easily angered,*
> *Love keeps no record of wrongs.*
> *Love does not delight in evil*
> *Love rejoices with the truth.*
> *Love always protects,*
> *Love always trusts,*
> *Love always hopes,*
> *Love always perseveres.*
> *Love never fails.*

Agape Love Commanded:

Jesus gave a new commandment to His disciples before going to Calvary in John 13:34: *"Love one another; as I have loved you."* This is not just a brotherly love, but agape love, the God-kind of love, the self-sacrificing love that sent Christ to die for sinners. This type of love can only come through believers who are Spirit-controlled.

There was a lawyer who once came to Jesus and asked, "Which is the greatest commandment in the Law?" Jesus said unto him, *"Love the Lord your God with all your heart and with all your soul and with all your mind. And the second is like it: Love your neighbor as yourself. All the Law and the Prophets hang on these two commandments"* (Matthew 22:37-40). That is to say, the summation of what is in the Old Testament is love toward God and man. This tells us the importance of agape love. Therefore, love must be the motivation for everything we do. And Jesus demonstrated it by going to the cross for us when we never cared or knew Him (Romans 5:8).

Love Is the Mark of a Disciple:

Believers were first called Christians in Antioch. Why? Because of the Christ-like love the people saw among the followers of Jesus. Barnabas and Paul stayed a whole year in Antioch teaching and preaching the Word of God, and the result was that the church started behaving like Christ, so they called them Christians. John the beloved said, *"He who does not love does not know God, for God is love"* (1 John 4:8). Jesus also reminded His disciples that when the people saw their display of this God-kind of love toward each other, they would know they were His disciples (John 13:35). This is the type of love that will help and encourage us to obey Jesus (John 14:15; 1 John 5:1-2).

Agape Love toward Our Enemies:

It is agape love that helps us go beyond our anger and allows us to forgive those who trespass against us because we realize how much God has forgiven us. Jesus in His teaching at Mount Olive said, *"But I say unto you, Love your enemies, bless them that curse you, do good to them that hate you, and pray for them which despitefully use you, and persecute you"* (Matthew 5:44; Luke 6:27-28).

Love Corrects:

Agape love does not mean we don't correct or discipline. Your true friend will correct you or point out an error he sees in you because he wants to help you. Our loving God corrects us for our own good. *"As many as I love, I rebuke and chasten: be zealous therefore, and repent"* (Revelation 3:19).

Joy

The second characteristic of the fruit is joy. The word "joy" comes from "rejoice," which means "to feel great delight, to be glad." Joy is not the same as happiness because it does not depend on a state of well-being or a pleasurable or satisfying experience. Joy is the fruit of the Spirit; therefore it does not change with outward circumstances.

Happiness depends on the circumstances you are in now. You cannot feel happy if you are not happy. You don't feel happy if you are sick or a member of your family is sick. You cannot make yourself happy if you don't have money to buy food for your family.

Happiness follows your present situation. If you get a promotion, you are happy. But joy does not depend on what is happening now: it is the fruit of the Spirit. The Apostle James said, *"My brethren, count it all joy when ye fall into divers temptations"* (James 1:2).

Kay Warren, the wife of Rick Warren, defines joy as "the settled assurance that God is in control of all the details of my life, the quiet confidence that ultimately everything is going to be alright, and the determined choice to praise God in every situation." This means that even when things are not yet all right, your joy is still there, because your faith is in the unfailing God.

Joy Maintained by Faith:

The lack of faith is what hinders the manifestation of perpetual joy in a believer's life. The opposite of faith is fear. Where there is fear, people tend to worry and doubt, and in such an atmosphere, full joy cannot manifest. Remember, when the storm rose on the sea, the disciples were fearful, and Jesus rebuked them and spoke to the wind, and immediately the storm stopped. Jesus then said to them, "Why are you fearful, you of little faith?" The lack of faith will prevent your abiding **Joy.**

Worry will also hinder joy. Jesus reminds us not to become worried about our daily needs. He of course did not say we should not work, but if you are not lazy and you do your best, then leave the rest in the hands of God. Jesus told His disciples that God provides for the fowls of the air that do not sow nor reap, yet they do not lack food; how much more you that are made in His image? To grow in faith we must feed on the Word daily (Romans 10:17). In Romans 15:13, Paul prays that God will fill the believers' hearts with all joy through the power of the Holy Spirit.

Hope Encourages Joy:

Because of the joy that was ahead of Jesus Christ, we are told in Hebrews 12:2, He endured the cross, not caring about the shame. And now He is seated at the right hand of the throne of God and will one day set His kingdom over the whole earth.

The apostles were arrested twice in Jerusalem and ordered not to speak in the name of Jesus. The second time they were brought before the Sanhedrin, they were flogged. They were not discouraged, but went rejoicing because they had been counted worthy of suffering disgrace for Jesus (Acts 5:41). Why? Because of the joy ahead of them. They followed in the footsteps of our Lord, as in Hebrews 12:2.

Because of the joy ahead, you say to yourself, whatever the trials may be, you already know the end; it shall be well and will be to the glory of God. You recognize that the joy of the Lord is your strength! Paul said, *"But none of these things move me, neither count I my life dear unto myself, so that I might finish my course with joy, and the ministry, which I have received of the Lord Jesus, to testify the gospel of the grace of God"* (Acts 20:24). Instead of hindering our faith, adversity actually enhances our joy. When Paul and Silas faced adversity in the jail at Philippi, with their feet in the stocks, they had been dragged to the marketplace and stripped and beaten unjustly, but at midnight they began to pray and sang hymns to God, and suddenly a violent earthquake shook the foundation of the prison and the doors automatically opened. How could they be singing in the face of such adversity? Because of the joy that was set before them.

Peace

Peace is an inner repose and tranquility in the midst of turmoil; it is a virtue that Christ gives. The Greek word *eirene* is translated as "peace," and its equivalent in Hebrew is *Shalom*, which means "completeness, soundness, or tranquility." Peace is more than just the absence of conflict. It is an inward assurance that does not depend on outward circumstances: an assurance deeply rooted in God, who is in control of your life, and His promise that says, "I will never leave you nor forsake you."

People long for peace, either inner or external peace. You want to have peace in your home, peace with your neighbors, and peace in the nation. But much of the news we hear or see is quite disturbing and could erode peace. Just recently, several people were shot dead by a lone gunman at a community college in Oregon, and not too long ago, some Christians in a Bible study were killed by another gunman. For decades, many US presidents and the United Nations have worked tirelessly to bring peace into the Middle East, but with little or no success. Families have been displaced from their countries to become refugees in other nations due to lack of peace.

In some homes, the children are settled and happy, but suddenly their parents can no longer live together, and so they divorce and the peaceful environment the children were used to is gone. I asked a young mother who recently divorced, "Why can't you reconcile with your husband?" She said, "I just want to have my peace." A survey taken some years ago revealed that most men prefer peace at home rather than a well-furnished home or an upper-class house without peace.

Then why can't we just have peace? The problem is that we are looking for peace in the wrong places. The Prince of Peace is forsaken. Isaiah foretold the coming Prince of Peace who would be born in Bethlehem. When He was born, the angel of the Lord proclaimed the good news to the shepherds and said, "Glory to God in the highest, and on earth peace, good will toward men." Before Jesus the Prince of Peace went to the cross, He told His disciples, *"Peace I leave with you, my peace I give unto you: not as the world giveth, give I unto you. Let not your heart be troubled, neither let it be afraid"* (John 14:27).

The peace that Jesus offers is peace with God. Man was at enmity with God because of disobedience which led to sin, but Christ through his death and resurrection restored the relationship or peace between us and God. This peace comes by putting your faith in the only Son of God. When we have peace with God, then it is possible to have inner peace with yourself and peace with your neighbors. This is the kind of peace Paul is talking about in Galatians 5:22, which is the fruit of the Spirit.

God promised in Isaiah 26:3 to give us perfect peace because we trust in Him. In Philippians, God also promised to guard our hearts and minds with peace that surpasses all understanding. These promises are not affected by outward circumstance, meaning no matter what situation you are in, you can be at peace.

Patience (Longsuffering)

The King James Version uses the word "longsuffering" for patience. Patience is forbearance or tolerance. It is the quality of endurance under provocation without seeking revenge even when mistreated.

We all love and praise patience, but we find it hard to practice. You want the driver behind you to be patient with you, but find it hard to be patient with the one in front of you. As children, we are told to be patient and we hear the saying, "The patient dog eats the fattest bone." You've probably heard the saying that you don't pray to God to give you patience or else He might give you something to try your patience. Charles H. Spurgeon said, *"Patience is better than wisdom: an ounce of patience is worth a pound of brains. All men praise patience, but few enough can practice it; it is a medicine which is good for all diseases, and therefore every old woman recommends it; but it is not every garden that grows the herbs to make it with."*

God Is Patient:

The Bible tells us in 2 Peter 3:9 that God is longsuffering toward us, not willing that any should perish, but that all should come to repentance. God has been patient with mankind. He waits patiently for us to come and receive the salvation that He offers through Jesus Christ. He continues to speak to the hearts of people, even when they are rebellious and stubborn, until His light shines in their hearts.

God is slow to anger and abounding in steadfast love, forgiving iniquity and transgression. Being slow to anger means God is patient or longsuffering with us. Patience does not mean that you never become angry; anger is not always wrong. Since sin is abhorrence to God, it causes Him to be angry, but He is slow to anger. People can be quick to anger and at the same time slow to release it. And what happens when you do not get rid of it quickly? It ferments and turns into bitterness, resentment, and retaliation. The book of Proverbs says, *"A hot-tempered man stirs up dissension, but a patient man calms a quarrel"* (Proverbs 15:1, NIV).

Patience Is a Choice:

A little patience will save us from a lot of trouble. Accidents occur because one driver is not patient and runs the red light and regrets not being patient. In general, people do not want to wait, but patience requires waiting, and our culture and the advances in technology do not help us learn patience. We have instant coffee, frozen dinners, fast food, wireless Internet, and freeway express lanes, and it's difficult to wait. I remember how in the early '80s I had to wait in line for more than three hours at the bank to get money for my family for food. We never had options then as we have today. Thank God for the advances in technology but in life not all things are express or overnight delivery.

The Bible gives us several stories of people who exercised patience in trials or adversity as well as those who were impatient and the consequences. Job was one who went through much tragedy. He lost his wealth (Job 1:14-17), his family (Job 1:18-19), and his health (Job 2:7). But we are told that with all these things that came on Job, instead of complaining and murmuring, he fell down upon the ground and worshipped God (Job 1:20-21). For his patience, we read that the Lord blessed the latter end of Job more than his beginning (Job 42:12). In the New Testament, James commended Job's patience: *"Behold, we count them happy which endure. Ye have heard of the patience of Job, and have seen the end of the Lord; that the Lord is very pitiful, and of tender mercy"* (James 5:11).

David is another person who in his time of trouble waited patiently for the Lord and cried onto Him. And what did he get? The Lord answered his prayer (Psalm 18:6; 40:1).

In the book of Numbers we read the story of Moses the leader of Israel, who was described as the meekest man upon the face of the earth, but lost his patience with the children of Israel. At Kadesh, there was no water for the children of Israel to drink, and they complained, *"And wherefore have ye made us to come up out of Egypt, to bring us in unto this evil place? it is no place of seed, or of figs, or of vines, or of pomegranates; neither is there any water to drink"* (Numbers 20:5). Out of frustration, Moses hit the rock with his staff twice and called the people rebels instead of speaking to the rock for water as commanded by God. Because of his lack of patience with the people, God did not allow him to enter the promised land.

There is a saying among the Yorubas of Nigeria that *"igbe esinsin ko ni ki alapata ma ta tire"*—that is, the noise of the flies does not stop the butcher man (meat seller) from selling his meat. If a meat seller pays attention to the noise of the flies, he will be frustrated and will leave. No matter how good you are, people will have something to complain about, so don't let them distract you from your goal or from obeying your God.

Saul, the first king over Israel, lost the establishment of his kingship in part due to lack of patience. He could no longer wait for Samuel the priest, who was God's right person to proffer the burnt offering. Just as he ended the offering, Samuel came. His reason was that he felt compelled when he saw his people scattered and Samuel did not come at the set time. Do you feel compelled to take action when you feel God is delaying? What did Saul get? *"Thou hast done foolishly: thou hast not kept the commandment of the LORD thy God, which he commanded thee: for now would the LORD have established thy kingdom upon Israel for ever. But now thy kingdom shall not continue"* (1 Samuel 13:13-14).

The Apostle James illustrated patience with the example of a husbandman or farmer (James 5:7). A farmer knows that he cannot hurry the harvest, and so he exercises patience until the due time. He plows, plants his seed, pulls weeds, and eventually harvests. He knows that the harvest will come if he will just be patient. So he watches for problems that need solving while he waits for his precious crops to grow.

Patience with Others:

Paul admonishes believers to bear with one another in love (Ephesians 4:2). We have seen earlier that love is patient. In 1 Thessalonians 5:14, Paul urges believers to be patient with everyone, and in particular with people who are sometimes difficult to express patience with, such as people who are idle (lazy), timid (shy), and weak. Paul realized we can be patient when it is easy.

Kindness

The King James Version translated the Greek word *chrestotes* as "gentleness," but it can also mean "kindness, goodness, integrity, or benignity." Kindness is benevolence in action such as God expressed toward mankind by providing salvation for us.

Kindness is easier to recognize than it is to define. We all want to be treated with courtesy and kindness. Paul describes love as patient and kind (1 Corinthians 13:4). That is to say, you cannot easily differentiate the characteristics of the fruit of the Spirit. They are all interwoven or blended together to make the fruit complete and tasty. When you talk of kindness, love is equally involved, and vice versa. Kindness is an active expression of love toward God and others, while patience is love forbearing under provocation.

These passages of Scripture below show us God's kindness toward undeserving people.

"He has shown kindness by giving you rain from heaven and crops in their seasons; He provides you with plenty of food and fills your hearts with joy" (Acts 14:17, NIV).

"At one time we too were foolish, disobedient, deceived and enslaved by all kinds of passions and pleasures. We lived in malice and envy, being hated and hating one another. But when the kindness and love of God our Savior appeared, He saved us, not because of righteous things we had done, but because of His mercy. He saved us through the washing of rebirth and renewal by the Holy Spirit" (Titus 3:3-5, NIV).

God gives rain and sun for our crops to grow and provide food even to people who have never appreciated Him or thanked Him. He meets both their spiritual and physical needs.

Jesus Demonstrated Kindness:

People from all walks of life were attracted to Jesus because of His kindness. On multiple occasions, kindness made Jesus stop what He was doing and help others in need. Jesus saw the multitude of people wondering around like sheep without a shepherd, and we are told that He was moved with compassion and began to teach them and heal them (Mark 6:34). There were instances when He fed thousands of people; this is a demonstration of kindness.

Kindness Illustrated:

Jesus illustrated kindness with the outstanding parable of the "Good Samaritan." In this parable Jesus shows not only whom to be kind to, but what can hinder us from showing kindness to people. This parable is recorded in Luke 10, and it was told in response to a question by a Jewish lawyer. This Pharisee expert in the law came to Jesus trying to tempt Him, and asked, "What must I do to inherit eternal life?" Jesus responded by asking him what was written in the law. The lawyer answered, "Love the Lord your God with all your heart and with all your soul and with all your strength and with all your mind; and, your neighbor as yourself." To the credit of the lawyer, Jesus said, "You have answered correctly, but go and do what you have just said and you will live."

The Bible says the lawyer, wanting to justify himself, asked, "Who is my neighbor?" This question immediately reveals what was in his heart, because if he had loved all people as himself, he wouldn't be asking who his neighbor was. Jesus proceeded to relate the parable of a man who was going down from Jerusalem to Jericho, and fell into the hands of robbers. He was beaten, stripped, and left half dead. A priest came by him and simply passed by on the other side, and so did a Levite. But a Samaritan came where the man was, and had pity on him, dressed his wounds, and took him to a caretaker. He paid for the cost and promised to come back and pay any extra expense for this man who was robbed and beaten. Jesus now asked the lawyer, "Which of these three do you think was a neighbor to the man who fell into the hands of the robbers?" The lawyer answered, "The one who had mercy on him."

In this parable, Jesus teaches us two very important things: First, our neighbor is anyone in need of help to whom we show kindness by our action. The man who fell into the hands of the robbers needed help or he would die. Both the priest and the Levite saw him but simply passed by. Remember, these were the elite or upper-class people within the Jewish community at the time. Samaritans were regarded as inferior and hated by the Jewish people at the time because they were half Jews, but it was one of those Samaritans that stopped and cared for this man in need.

Secondly, pride breeds unkindness. The priest and the Levite, being in the upper class of their society, did not see themselves coming down to the level of this poor fellow who needed help, and they simply passed by him. In Philippians 2 we are told to have the mind of Christ, that is, humility. Jesus the Son of God made Himself of no reputation, and took upon Himself the form of a servant, and was made in the likeness of men. *"And being found in fashion as a man, he humbled himself, and became obedient unto death, even the death of the cross"* (Philippians 2:7-8).

As believers, we are told to clothe ourselves with compassion, kindness, humility, gentleness, and patience (Colossians 3:12). Without these virtues the world will not respond favorably to our preaching – sometimes the most effective witness is kindness. The world is full of angry responses, but needs gentle words. *"A gentle answer turns away wrath, but a harsh word stirs up anger"* (Proverbs 15:18, NIV). Our kindness should be unbiased and demonstrated to all people, irrespective of their tribe or race.

Goodness

Goodness refers to the state of being good, moral excellence, virtue, kindness, benevolence, or reaching out to others to do good when they don't deserve it. It is a Christ-like life and conduct. God is the source of our goodness. He told Moses, *"The Lord God, merciful and gracious, longsuffering, and abundant in goodness and truth"* (Exodus 34:6). Psalm 25:8 says, *"Good and upright is the Lord: therefore will he teach sinners in the way."*

Goodness, like the other characteristics of the fruit of the Spirit, is not manufactured by us. It shows in our lives as we align ourselves with the source of goodness. The book of James says, *"Every good gift and every perfect gift is from above, and cometh down from the Father of lights"* (James 1:17). When a certain ruler came to Jesus and said, *"Good Master, what shall I do to inherit eternal life? And Jesus said unto him, Why callest thou me good? none is good, save one, that is, God"* (Luke 18:18-19).

In the first place, the ruler realized that Jesus was good by His life and conduct, but Jesus wanted him to know the source of goodness. And that is God, but through the Holy Spirit. As we remain in Christ the Vine, we the branches bear the fruit. It normally takes time for the fruit to mature and ripen on the branches, and it will take time for the Christ-like character to form and mature in us. However, we must continue to get nourishment through the study of God's Word. Then others will see our good works, as the ruler saw in Jesus, and the praise will be to our Father in heaven (Matthew 5:16).

Goodness Is from Inside:

Jesus said, *"O generation of vipers, how can ye, being evil, speak good things? For out of the abundance of the heart the mouth speaks. A good man out of the good treasure of the heart brings forth good things: and an evil man out of the evil treasure brings forth evil things"* (Matthew 12:34-35). It is what is inside of a man that comes out of his mouth. Have you ever made a small joke to someone and suddenly he explodes? You wonder how your statement could have caused so much trouble. He was nursing some resentment in his heart toward you, and what you thought was a small thing simply triggered what was inside. Most people hide their feelings and you cannot see it on the outside. If you have two bottles, one filled with water and the other with sulphuric acid, they look alike from the outside, but if you shake the bottles and let them spill on your clothes, you will see the big difference. The water will not destroy your clothes, but the acid will.

In general, most people want to be good and to live a good life. However, goodness is a spiritual thing. It is not something simply produced by you. Having goods or feeling good or looking good is not goodness. But when you are good inside, it translates to goodness shown outwardly. The fruit of goodness will inspire people to do what is best for others without counting the cost.

Imitate God:

There are people who compare themselves to others and say, "I am good because I am better than that person." Remember, others are not the standard of goodness: God is. Because of the goodness of God, He meets the needs of both good and evil. Jesus teaches us to love our enemies, and do good to them, and lend to them without expecting to get anything back; then our reward will be great, and we will be sons of the Most High, because He is kind to the ungrateful and wicked (Luke 6:35).

Faithfulness

Faithfulness is a virtue of the fruit of the Spirit. It is a quality that makes a person steadfast, constant, or trustworthy. This comes as we allow the Holy Spirit to work in us. The eleventh chapter of the book of Hebrews, usually called the "Hall of Fame of Faith," gives us a list of people in the Old

Testament who were faithful to God. The list starts with Abel, whose sacrifice was accepted by God because through faith he brought a more excellent offering than his brother Cain. Through faith, Sarah the wife of Abraham received strength to conceive and delivered the promised child when it was humanly impossible because she was past childbearing age; the Bible says, *"She judged Him faithful who had promised"* (Hebrews 11:11). There were those tortured, and even killed, refusing to be released, so that they might obtain a better resurrection. The faithful take God as the truth, and no matter what is happening in their lives, it does not change their belief.

God's Faithfulness:

The Psalmist says, *"I will sing of the mercies of the LORD forever: with my mouth will I make known thy faithfulness to all generations. For I have said, Mercy shall be built up for ever: thy faithfulness shalt thou establish in the very heavens"* (Psalm 89:1-2). God is faithful even when we are faithless because He cannot deny Himself (2 Timothy 2:13). Whatever He says He will do, He will, even when we feel He is slow and give up on Him. Our God is steadfast. He is faithful and just to forgive our sins when we confess to Him (1 John 1:9).

Faithfulness to God:

The question we should ask ourselves is: "Am I reciprocating God's faithfulness?" Many people believe in God's faithfulness to grant them eternal life, but fail to remain faithful to Him. How do we remain faithful to Him? We do that through obedience to His Word. Jesus says, *"If you love Me, keep My commandments"* (John 14:15). And Jesus sums up the commandments as, *"Love the Lord your God with all your heart, with all your soul, with all your strength, and with all your mind, and your neighbor as yourself."* Obedience demonstrates faithfulness and disobedience demonstrates unfaithfulness.

In Matthew 25, Jesus used the parable of the talents to illustrate faithfulness. The person who was given five talents of money by his master used it and gained five more, and another given two talents gained two more. But the person who was given one talent went and dug a hole in the ground and hid his master's money. Remember, these servants were given talents of money according to their abilities. When the master came back and they each rendered their accounts, the master commended the ones who received five and two talents and said, *"Well done, good and faithful servant! You have been faithful with a few things; I will put you in charge of many things. Come and share your master's happiness"* (Matthew 25:21). But the one who received one talent and hid it in the ground received condemnation from his master: *"You wicked and slothful servant."*

Are you faithful to God with what He has given to you? Do you give the tithe of what He has given you? In Malachi 3:8, God asked, *"Will a man rob God? Yet you have robbed Me!"* But you say, "In what way have we robbed You?" In tithes and offerings. Not returning back a tenth of what God gives you is unfaithfulness.

Faithfulness to Each Other:

You probably have heard people say, "I will be there," but you never see them and they may not care to call. And when some people say something, others who know them very well will sometimes say, "Please don't rely on their words." That is to say, they are not trustworthy or faithful. If you cannot be faithful to people that you see face to face, you will find it hard to be faithful to God.

Paul talks about faithfulness in our relationships in Ephesians 5: husband and wife, parent and child, employee and employer. It is almost daily news these days to hear or read about couples divorcing, especially celebrities. The majority of the divorces center on unfaithfulness—extramarital relationships. Remember, faithfulness is a characteristic of the fruit of the Spirit, and we cannot bear this fruit by our own effort. This will require feeding on the Word of God, praying, and being an active member of a local church.

Gentleness

Gentleness means meekness. It is a disposition to be meek, kind, and indulgent. It does not mean weakness, as some people think. Actually, it is a restrained power. It is also a mark of one who is submissive to God's Word. He is teachable because of his submissiveness to God. Psalm 25:9 says, *"The meek will he guide in judgment: and the meek will he teach his way."* He is also considerate when disciplining others (Galatians 6:1).

Gentleness shows humility. In fact, without humility you cannot be gentle. Jesus demonstrated the greatest humility ever known to man. Hear what Paul said about His humility: *"Who, being in the form of God, thought it not robbery to be equal with God: But made himself of no reputation, and took upon him the form of a servant, and was made in the likeness of men: And being found in fashion as a man, he humbled himself, and became obedient unto death, even the death of the cross"* (Philippians 2:6-8).

Jesus washing the feet of His disciples was another display of gentleness. He as the master had to pull His garment aside, pour water into a basin, take a towel, and start washing their feet. The natural thing would have been the opposite, but humility and meekness made him do it. He then reminded the disciples and every believer that *"If I then, your Lord and Master, have washed your feet; ye also ought to wash one another's feet"* (John 13:14).

The meekness of Jesus is well described in a hymn titled "I Want to Be Like Jesus" (Redemption Hymnal, Appendix 62).

I want to be like Jesus,
So lowly and so meek;
For no one marked an angry word,
That ever heard Him speak.

I want to be like Jesus,
So frequently in prayer;
Alone upon the mountain top,
He met His Father there.

I want to be like Jesus;
I never, never find
That He, though persecuted, was
To any one unkind.

Stanza one describes Him as lowly and meek—that is, humble and gentle. In Matthew 11:29, Jesus said, *"Take my yoke upon you, and learn of me; for I am meek and lowly in heart: and ye shall find rest unto your souls."* And in Matthew 21:5, we read, *"Tell ye the daughter of Sion, Behold, thy King cometh unto thee, meek, and sitting upon an ass, and a colt the foal of an ass."*

How was Jesus able to be lowly and gentle? Stanza two tells us, "So frequently in prayer; Alone upon the mountain top, He met His Father there." Prayer is essential to bearing and showing forth the fruit of the Holy Spirit. Prayer cultivates a deep relationship with the heavenly Father, and there He teaches us His way (Psalm 25:9). Moses was described as the meekest man upon the face of the earth. Why? Moses spent quality time with God, and then God made His ways known unto him, but only His acts unto the children of Israel.

Meekness is not self-aggrandizing. Most people who get irritated easily and become angry do that because of pride. They think the world revolves around them, so they say to themselves, "Either my way or no other ways." C. S. Lewis said, "Pride leads to every other vice: It is the complete anti-God state of mind."

The Bible teaches us that we should do nothing through strife or vainglory; but in lowliness of mind we should esteem others better than ourselves (Philippians 2:3). Now Jesus offers us the chance to bear His fruit of gentleness. We must allow the Holy Spirit to do His work in us, and our lives will be filled with meekness.

Paul teaches gentleness towards other brethren who have fallen into sin in Galatians 6:1: *"If a man be overtaken in a fault, ye which are spiritual, restore such a one in the spirit of meekness."* Gentleness here does not mean we do not point out what God says about a particular sin. It does not mean we go easy and leave the impression that we are trying to justify a sinful act. We are not to be soft in such a way that the sinner does not realize that what he has done is against God. We confront such a person with the intent to restore him, in love, and to encourage him to live a life that pleases God.

Self-Control

Self-control is called temperance in the King James Version. It denotes self-mastery or the art of curbing fleshly impulses. The Bible says, *"Like a city whose walls are broken down is a man who lacks self-control"* (Proverbs 25:28, NIV).

From time immemorial, man has not been good at mastering fleshly impulses, desires, or passions. Without the manifestation of the fruit of the Spirit in your life, you may easily yield to the flesh or passion. What led to sin in the Garden of Eden? It was lack of self-control. *"The woman saw that the tree was good for food, and that it was pleasant to the eyes, and a tree to be desired to make one wise, she took of the fruit thereof, and did eat"* (Genesis 3:6).

It seems many find it difficult to learn from other believers who have fallen into certain shameful sins. I remember some years back when certain great men of God fell into sexual sin and financial embezzlement; they came on television crying in public. What an embarrassing and shameful thing to watch! But no sooner had that happened than another believer fell into the same kind of sin. There was also a high political leader who was investigating his colleague for sexual immorality, but at the same time was sleeping with someone else's wife. No wonder Jesus asked the woman caught in adultery, "Where are your accusers?" Jesus was probably writing the different kinds of sins the accusers were guilty of in the sand, and when they saw their own sin, they simply disappeared.

It is not just unbelievers who struggle daily with self-control. Believers do too. We may ask ourselves, "Why can't I just control my inordinate appetite or desire?" It might be in the area of overeating, pornography, anger, gossiping, or the like. How can we have victory over these things? The fruit of the Spirit, which is the life of Christ in us, must continually manifest.

Self-control is the last of the virtues of the fruit of the Spirit as listed in the text, and it is obvious that without self-control you cannot consistently display love, joy, peace, patience, kindness, goodness, faithfulness, and gentleness. Jesus said, "Without Me you can do nothing," and that is why He said, "Abide in Me," because the branch cannot bear fruit of itself unless it abides in the vine. For us to have self-control, we must let the Holy Spirit take control, because the natural man is selfish and wants to be in control. Yield to the Holy Spirit and let Him be the driver each day of your life.

"But the fruit of the Spirit is love, joy, peace, patience, kindness, goodness, faithfulness, gentleness and self-control. Against such things there is no law" (Galatians 5:22-23, NIV).

www.ingramcontent.com/pod-product-compliance
Lightning Source LLC
Chambersburg PA
CBHW071503080526
44587CB00014B/2202